SCHOLASTIC

50

MATHS LESSONS FOR LESS ABLE LEARNERS

- Tricky topics covered
- Ideas to build confidence
- Photocopiable activities

AGES
5-7

Louise Carruthers

Credits

Author
Louise Carruthers

Illustrations
Peter Curry

Editor
Sally Gray

Series Designer
Micky Pledge

Assistant Editor
Victoria Paley

Designer
Micky Pledge

Text © 2006 Louise Carruthers
© 2006 Scholastic Ltd

Designed using Adobe InDesign

Published by Scholastic Ltd
Villiers House
Clarendon Avenue
Leamington Spa
Warwickshire CV32 5PR

www.scholastic.co.uk

Printed by Bell and Bain Ltd, Glasgow.

2 3 4 5 6 7 8 9   6 7 8 9 0 1 2 3 4 5

British Library Cataloguing-in-Publication Data
A catalogue record for this book is available from the British Library.

ISBN 0-439-965-195
ISBN 978-0439-965194

Contents

4 INTRODUCTION

6 NNS GRID

10 MENTAL MATHS STARTERS

28 DOTTY THE DOG

30 ONE MORE MAX

32 ONE MORE, ONE LESS

34 RACE TO 100

36 TEN MORE MACHINE

38 SWIM TO SHORE

40 MRS ODD AND MR EVEN

42 POP TO THE SHOP

44 AT THE BANK

46 STAR COLLECTOR

48 ZERO THE HERO!

50 SNAKE RACE

52 PIGGY IN THE MIDDLE

54 TRAFFIC JAM

56 YOUNGEST TO OLDEST

58 PIZZA TOPPINGS

60 BIRTHDAY CANDLES

62 HOW MANY APPLES?

64 LARGEST FIRST

66 LUCKY DIP

68 HOOK A DUCK

70 TEN LITTLE LOLLIPOPS

72 COLOURFUL CATERPILLARS

74 SHOPKEEPER'S CHANGE

76 NEAREST TEN

78 THAT'S MAGIC! (1)

80 THAT'S MAGIC! (2)

82 LADYBIRD DOUBLES

84 DOUBLE DECKER

86 FIVE LITTLE FISH

88 NEAR DOUBLES

90 TAKE ME HOME

92 BACK TO TEN

94 ADDING 11

96 FIVE AND A BIT

98 AFTERNOON TEA

100 MONEY BAGS

102 AT THE CAFÉ

104 CHANGE MACHINE

106 STAMP COLLECTOR

108 FEELING FRUITY

110 WHO HAS THE LONGEST SCARF?

112 ARE WE NEARLY THERE YET?

114 WHAT'S YOUR FAVOURITE?

116 PARTY FOOD

118 WHAT'S THE TIME MR WOLF?

120 WHERE'S THE BEAR?

122 MUSICAL SHAPES

124 COUNTING CORNERS

126 CAT AND MOUSE

About the series

50 Maths Lessons for Less Able Learners is a series of three books designed for teachers and learning support assistants working with lower ability children within the daily maths lesson. Each book covers a two-year span of the primary age range: KS1 5-7 and KS2 7-9 and 9-11.

Each title consists of 50 oral and mental starter activities and 50 lesson plans each with an accompanying photocopiable activity page. The activities cover many of the Key objectives in the National Numeracy Strategy's Framework for Teaching Mathematics.

The lesson plans and accompanying photocopiable activities are designed to:
● Support less confident learners with a range of key mathematical concepts.
● Motivate children with engaging activities and games.
● Suggest ways to modify activities to address different learning styles.
● Fit into the individual teacher's existing planning for mathematics.

How to use this book

This book begins with a detailed Objectives grid, which gives an overview of the objectives addressed by each lesson. Teachers can also use this grid to track backwards to identify appropriate objectives from previous years where necessary.

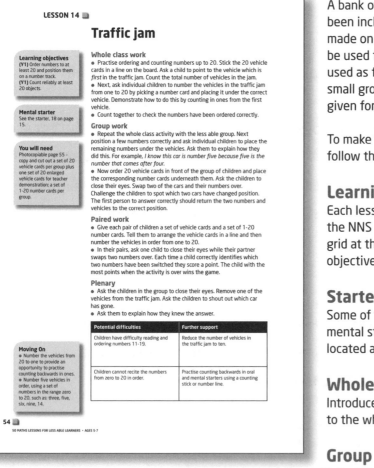

A bank of 50 oral and mental starters has then been included. Links to appropriate starters are made on each lesson plan. However, they can also be used flexibly as required. They might also be used as focused oral assessment activities with small groups. A set of target questions has been given for this purpose.

To make the book easy to use all 50 lesson plans follow the same format.

Learning objectives

Each lesson is written to address one or more of the NNS objectives from either Years 1 and 2. The grid at the front of the book tracks back to show objectives from Reception.

Starter activity

Some of the lessons have a suggested linked mental starter activity from the bank of starters located at the front of the book (pages 10-27)

Whole class work

Introduces the context and concept of each lesson to the whole class.

Group work

This details the teaching activity to be undertaken by groups of less able learners led by either the class teacher or a teaching assistant. Various teaching strategies are used and knowledge and skills are presented creatively to engage children and appeal to different learning styles. Opportunities for children to talk about their work and explain their ideas and understanding are

4 📋

offered throughout. Activities are designed to build on what children know – the aim being to build confidence. Emphasis is placed on active participation by the children through, for example, the use of games and role play. Suggested questions and opportunities for teacher interventions are also included (see below for further information).

Independent/paired work
Where appropriate an individual or paired activity is suggested. These provide opportunities for the less confident children to work with greater independence. The activities suggested are intended to reinforce and consolidate the learning that takes place in the teacher led part of the lesson and include a variety of games, reinforcement activities or problems to solve. Many of the activities can be easily adapted to use on more than one occasion.

Plenary
Where possible the plenary offers an opportunity to reflect on less confident children's understanding of the lesson objective.

Potential difficulties and further support
This grid outlines potential difficulties children might experience. Suggestions for further differentiating the activities for children who require extra support are provided, as well as notes on adapting the activities for children's different learning styles.

Moving on
At the end of each plan, ideas are included for how to progress children who have met the objectives.

Interventions
The NNS suggests that 'as far as possible, children should work together'. This inclusive approach therefore requires a variety of intervention techniques for children working significantly below expected levels of attainment. The NNS identifies three waves of possible interventions, as outlined above. These include whole class teaching for all children (wave 1), interventions in small groups with the teacher or learning support assistants (wave 2) and targeted interventions with individuals (wave 3). Each lesson reflects this approach with opportunities for different types of intervention offered throughout.

The Broad Curriculum
The *50 Maths Lessons for Less Able Learners* series sits comfortably within the principles of 'Excellence and Enjoyment' (DfES, 2004), giving renewed emphasis to inclusive practice and flexible curriculum planning.

Ofsted's report for 2002 confirmed that the National Numeracy Strategy continues to have a positive impact on the teaching of pupils with special educational needs. Their report also confirms that almost all pupils with special educational needs are included in the daily mathematics lesson.

The *50 Maths Lessons* series features numerous activities that call on the child to apply knowledge and understanding to wider contexts, but within an environment tailored more to the needs of the less confident learner. Through skilful and timely intervention the child is likely to be well placed to benefit from this modified programme. At the same time, the incorporation of common themes and whole class activity minimises the possibility of the child feeling excluded or marginalised.

█ 5

Title of lesson	Tracking back Reception objectives	Year 1 objectives	Tracking forwards Year 2 objectives
1 Dotty the dog	● **Say and use the number names in order in familiar contexts.** ● **Count reliably up to 10 everyday objects.**	● Rrecite numbers in order to at least 20, from and back to zero. ● **Count reliably at least 20 objects.**	● Say the number names in order to at least 100, from and back to zero.
2 One more Max	● Recite the number names in order, continuing the count forwards or backwards from a given number.	● Count on and back in ones from any small number. ● **Within the range 0 to 30 say the number that is 1 more or less than any given number.**	● **Count on or back in ones, starting from any two-digit number.** ● Say the number that is 1 more or less than any given two-digit number.
3 One more, one less	● Recite the number names in order, continuing the count forwards or backwards from a given number.	● **Count on and back in ones from any small number.** ● **Within the range 0 to 30 say the number that is 1 more or less than any given number.**	● **Count on or back in ones, starting from any two-digit number.** ● Say the number that is 1 more or less than any given two-digit number.
4 Race to 100	● Count in tens.	● **Count in tens from and back to zero.**	● **Count on or back in tens, starting from any two-digit number.**
5 Ten more machine	● Count in tens.	● **Within the range 0 to 30 say the number that is 10 more or less than any given number.**	● **Count on or back in tens, starting from any two-digit number.** ● Say the number that is 10 more or less than any given two-digit number.
6 Swim to shore	● Count in tens.	● **Within the range 0 to 30 say the number that is 10 more or less than any given number.**	● Say the number that is 1 or 10 more or less than any given two-digit number. ● Use and begin to read the related vocabulary.
7 Mrs Odd and Mr Even	● Count in twos.	● Describe and extend number sequences. ● Count on in twos from 0 then 1, and begin to recognise odd or even numbers to about 20 as 'every other number'.	● Recognise odd and even numbers to at least 30.
8 Pop to the shop	● Count in twos.	● Describe and extend number sequences. ● Count on in twos.	● Recognise odd and even numbers to at least 30.
9 At the bank	● Count in tens. ● Count in ones.	● Begin to know what each digit in a two-digit number represents. ● Partition a 'teens' number into a multiple of ten and ones.	● Know what each digit in a two-digit number represents, including zero as a place holder.
10 Star collector	● Count in tens. ● Count in ones.	● Begin to know what each digit represents in numbers 10-20. ● Partition two-digit numbers into a multiple of ten and ones (TU).	● Know what each digit in a two-digit number represents, including zero as a place holder.
11 Zero the hero		● Begin to know what each digit in a two-digit number represents.	● Know what each digit in a two-digit number represents, including zero as a place holder.
12 Snake race	● **Use language such as more or less, greater or smaller,** to compare two numbers and say which is more or less.	● **Understand and use the vocabulary of comparing and ordering numbers.** ● Compare two familiar numbers and say which is more or less.	● Use and begin to read the vocabulary of comparing and ordering numbers. ● Compare two given two-digit numbers, say which is more or less.
13 Piggy in the middle	● **Use language such as more or less, greater or smaller,** to compare two numbers and say a number which lies between two given numbers.	● **Understand and use the vocabulary of comparing and ordering numbers.** ● Compare two familiar numbers and give a number which lies between them.	● Use and begin to read the vocabulary of comparing and ordering numbers. ● Compare two given two-digit numbers and give a number which lies between them.

Title of lesson	Tracking back Reception objectives	Year 1 objectives	Tracking forwards Year 2 objectives
14 Traffic jam	● Order a given set of numbers.	● **Order numbers from 0 to at least 20** and position them on a number track.	● **Order whole numbers to at least 100.**
15 Youngest to oldest	● Order a given set of numbers.	● **Order numbers from 0 to at least 20.**	● **Order whole numbers to at least 100.**
16 Pizza toppings	● **Begin to relate addition to combining two groups of objects,** counting all the objects.	● Begin to use the +, - and = signs to record mental calculations in a number sentence.	● **Use knowledge that addition can be done in any order to do mental calculations more efficiently.**
17 Birthday candles	● Separate a given number of objects into two groups.	● Begin to know addition facts for pairs of numbers with a total up to at least 10. ● Solve simple mathematical problems and puzzles.	● **Know by heart all addition and subtraction facts for each number to at least 10.**
18 How many apples?	● Begin to relate addition to counting on. ● Find a total by counting on when one group of objects is hidden.	● **Understand the operation of addition.**	● **Use knowledge that addition can be done in any order to do mental calculations more efficiently.**
19 Largest first	● Begin to relate addition to counting on. ● Find a total by counting on when one group of objects is hidden.	● Use knowledge that addition can be done in any order to do mental calculations more efficiently. For example: put the larger number first and count on in ones.	● **Use knowledge that addition can be done in any order.** Put the larger number first and count on.
20 Lucky dip (1)	● **Begin to relate addition to combining two groups of objects,** counting all the objects, extend to three groups of objects.	● Begin to recognise that more than two numbers can be added together. ● Begin to use the +, - and = signs to record mental calculations in a number sentence.	● Begin to add three single-digit numbers mentally or three two digit numbers with the help of apparatus.
21 Hook a duck	● **Begin to relate addition to combining two groups of objects,** counting all the objects, extend to three groups of objects.	● Begin to recognise that more than two numbers can be added together.	● Begin to add three single-digit numbers mentally or three two-digit numbers with the help of apparatus.
22 Ten little lollipops	● **Begin to relate subtraction to 'taking away'** and counting how many are left.	● **Understand the operation of subtraction as 'take away'.** ● Solve simple problems set in 'real life'.	● Use the - and = signs to record mental subtractions in a number sentence.
23 Colourful caterpillars	● Find out how many have been removed from a larger group of objects by counting up from a number.	● **Understand the operation of addition and of subtraction (as 'take away', 'difference' and 'how many more to make') and use the related vocabulary.**	● Find a small difference by counting up from the smaller to the larger number.
24 Shopkeeper's change	● Find out how many have been removed from a larger group of objects by counting up from a number.	● **Understand the operation of subtraction as 'difference'.**	● Find a small difference by counting up from the smaller to the larger number.
25 Nearest ten	● Count in tens.	● **Count on and back in tens from and back to zero.**	● Recognise multiples of 10. ● Round a number to the nearest 10.
26 That's magic (1)	● Partition a given number of objects into two groups.	● **Know by heart all pairs of numbers with a total of 10.**	● Know by heart all pairs of numbers that total 20.
27 That's magic (2)	● Partition a given number of objects into two groups.	● **Know by heart all pairs of numbers with a total of 10.**	● Know by heart all pairs of numbers that total 20.
28 Ladybird doubles	● **To begin to relate addition to combining two groups of objects.**	● Know by heart addition doubles of all numbers to at least 5.	● Know by heart doubles of all numbers to 10 and the corresponding halves.

Title of lesson	Tracking back Reception objectives	Year 1 objectives	Tracking forwards Year 2 objectives
29 Double decker	● To begin to relate addition to combining two groups of objects.	● Know by heart addition doubles of all numbers to at least 5.	● Know by heart doubles of all numbers to 10 and the corresponding halves.
30 Five little fish	● Partition a given number of objects into two groups.	● **Know by heart all pairs of numbers with a total of 10 and the corresponding subtraction facts.** ● Know addition facts for all pairs of numbers with a total up to at least 5.	● **Know by heart all addition and subtraction facts for each number to at least 10.**
31 Near doubles	● **Begin to relate addition to combining two groups of objects.**	● Identify near doubles using doubles already known, eg 6 + 5.	● Identify near doubles using doubles already known (eg 40 + 41).
32 Take me home		● Use known number facts and place value to add or subtract a pair of numbers mentally within the range 0 to 20.	● Know by heart all pairs of numbers that total 20. ● Extend understanding of the operations of addition and subtraction.
33 Back to ten	● In practical activities and discussion begin to use the vocabulary involved in adding and subtracting.	● **Understand the operations of addition and subtraction and use the related vocabulary.**	● Understand that subtraction is the inverse of addition.
34 Adding 11		● Use known number facts and place value to add a pair of numbers mentally. ● Add 9 to single-digit numbers by adding 10 then subtracting 1.	● Add/subtract 9 or 11: add/subtract 10 and adjust by 1.
35 Five and a bit	● Partition a given number of objects into two groups.	● Begin to partition into '5 and a bit' when adding 6, 7, 8 or 9, then recombine (eg 6 + 8 = 5 + 1 + 5 + 3 = 10 + 4 = 14).	● Partition into 5 and a bit when adding 6, 7, 8 or 9 then recombine.
36 Afternoon tea	● Use developing mathematical ideas and methods to solve practical problems involving counting and comparing in a real or role-play context.	● Solve simple word problems set in 'real life' contexts. ● **Explain methods and reasoning orally.** ● Choose and use appropriate number operations to solve problems.	● **Choose and use appropriate operations and efficient calculation strategies to solve problems.**
37 Money bags	● Sort coins, including the £1 and £2 coins.	● Recognise all coins.	● Recognise all coins and begin to use £/p notation.
38 At the café	● To use coins in role-play to pay and give change.	● Solve simple problems set in money contexts. ● **Use knowledge that addition can be done in any order to do mental calculations more efficiently.** ● Put the largest number first and count on in ones.	● Use mental addition and subtraction to solve simple money problems, using one or two steps. ● Find totals.
39 Change machine	● To use coins in role-play to pay and give change.	● To solve simple problems involving money and explain how the problem was solved. ● To give change from 10p.	● Use mental addition and subtraction to solve simple money problems, using one or two steps. ● Give change.
40 Stamp collector	● To use coins in role-play to pay and give change.	● Solve simple problems set in real life, money or measurement contexts. ● **Explain methods and reasoning orally.** ● Find totals and change from up to 20p.	● Use mental addition and subtraction to solve simple money problems, using one or two steps. ● Work out which coins to pay.

Title of lesson	Tracking back Reception objectives	Year 1 objectives	Tracking forwards Year 2 objectives
41 Feeling fruity	● **To use language such as heavier or lighter to compare two numbers or quantities.**	● Understand and use the vocabulary related to mass. ● Measure using uniform non-standard units.	● **Estimate, measure and compare masses using standard units.**
42 Who has the longest scarf?	● **Use developing mathematical ideas and methods to solve practical problems** involving comparing in a real or role-play context.	● **Suggest suitable uniform non-standard units to estimate, then measure a length.** ● **Explain methods and reasoning orally.**	● **Estimate, measure and compare lengths using standard units.** ● **Suggest units and equipment for measurements.**
43 Are we nearly there yet?	● **Use developing mathematical ideas and methods to solve practical problems** involving comparing in a real or role-play context.	● Read the time to the hour on analogue clocks. ● Solve simple problems set in 'real life' contexts.	● Use mental calculation strategies to solve measurement problems set in a variety of contexts.
44 What's your favourite...?	● Sort and match objects, pictures or children themselves, justifying the decisions made.	● Solve a given problem by sorting, classifying and organising information in simple ways. Discuss and explain results.	● Solve a given problem by sorting, classifying and organising information in a block graph. Discuss and explain results.
45 Party food	● Sort and match objects, pictures or children themselves, justifying the decisions made.	● Solve a given problem by sorting, classifying and organising information in simple ways. Discuss and explain results.	● Solve a given problem by sorting, classifying and organising information in a block graph. Discuss and explain results.
46 What's the time Mr Wolf?	● Begin to read o'clock time.	● Understand and use the vocabulary related to time. ● Read the time to the hour on analogue clocks.	● Read the time to the hour, half hour or quarter hour on an analogue clock and a 12-hour digital clock.
47 Where's the bear?	● Use everyday words to describe position, direction and movement.	● Use everyday language to describe position.	● Recognise whole, half and quarter turns, to the left or right, clockwise or anti-clockwise.
48 Musical shapes	● Use language such as circle or bigger to describe the shape and size of solids and flat shapes.	● **Use everyday language to describe features of familiar 3D and 2D shapes.**	● Sort shapes and describe some of their features
49 Counting corners	● Use language such as circle or bigger to describe the shape and size of solids and flat shapes.	● **Use everyday language to describe features of familiar 3D and 2D shapes.**	● Sort shapes and describe some of their features.
50 Cat and mouse	● **Use everyday words to describe position,** direction and movement	● Use everyday language to describe position, direction and movement. ● Make whole turns and half turns.	● Recognise whole, half and quarter turns, to the left or right, clockwise or anti-clockwise.

Mental Maths starters

1 Magic beans

What to do
- Explain that you are going to drop 'magic' beans, one by one, into the pot. Tell the children to close their eyes and count how many beans you drop into the pot *altogether*.
- Give each child a number fan and ask them to hold up their answer.
- Let children who answer correctly close their eyes and make a wish!

Target questions
- How could I make it easier/harder for you to count the beans?
- Why do we have to say the numbers in the same order when we count?
- When we count, which number tells us how many there are altogether?

2 Money box

What to do
- Hold up a handful of coins. Drop the coins into the money box, one at a time. Ask the class to tell you how much money is in the money box.
- Encourage the children to count in their heads. If necessary, remind the children to count in steps of two or ten.
- Tip the coins out of the money box and count them as a class.

Target questions
- Show me how to use your fingers to help you keep track of the number of coins I drop.
- Were the number names we said odd or even numbers?
- If I drop another 10p into the money box, how much money will there be altogether?

3 Where's the bear?

What to do
- Place the teddy bear somewhere in the classroom such as on a chair or next to the computer.
- Ask the question: *Where's the Bear?*
- Choose a child to describe where the bear is. If they use correct positional vocabulary they can decide where to move the bear to next.

Target questions
- Is the bear *on* the table or *under* the table?
- Is the bear *behind* the bookcase or *in front of* the bookcase?
- Can you tell me where to put the bear next?

Learning objective
(Y1) Know the days of the week/months of the year in order.

You will need
The playground.

4 Shout it out

What to do
- Split the class into two groups. Tell the children that you are going to find out which group can shout the loudest.
- Send the groups to stand at opposite sides of the playground.
- Tell one group to shout *Monday* as loudly as they can. The other group must then shout back *Tuesday* and so on. Give the loudest group three cheers.
- Repeat the activity starting from different days of the week, or months of the year.

Target questions
- What day/month is it today?
- Can you say the days of the week in order starting with Wednesday?
- Can you say the months of the year in order starting with July?

Learning objective
(Y1) Count on and back in ones from any small number.

You will need
A fancy box containing a shuffled set of 0-20 number cards.

5 Pass the parcel

What to do
- Sit or stand in a whole class circle.
- Explain that you would like the children to pass the box around the circle while counting from 1 to 20.
- Instruct the child holding the box when 20 is reached to open it, pick a card and read out the number.
- Count on in ones to 20 from the number that has been drawn from the box. At the same time, pass the box on around the circle.

Target questions
- What number will come next?
- Who do you think will be holding the box when we reach 20?
- Are the numbers we are saying getting larger or smaller?

Learning objective
(Y2) To practise rapid recall of a range of number facts.

You will need
A tambourine.

6 Musical number facts

What to do
- Ask: *What is half of 2?* Shake the tambourine. Explain that when the tambourine stops you would like everyone to shout out the answer.
- Shake the tambourine for as long as you feel is necessary.
- As the children become more confident recalling the number facts, reduce the thinking time you give the class. Strike the tambourine quickly and ask the children to shout the answer out straight away.

Target questions
- What is half of 10?
- If double 3 makes 6 what is half of 6?
- When you halve a number, is the answer larger or smaller than the start number?

<table>
<tr><td>

Learning objective
(Y1) To know by heart all addition facts for numbers up to and including 5.

</td></tr>
</table>

You will need
A bag of dominoes - each with a total of five spots or less.

7 Number bond dominoes

What to do
- Tell the children that you are going to time them to see how many domino totals they can correctly identify in two minutes.
- Take a domino out of the bag and hold it up for the class to look at. Conceal the domino again. Ask: *How many spots are on the domino altogether?*
- Repeat the activity later in the week. Challenge the group to improve their score.

Target questions
- How many spots are on each side of the domino?
- How many spots are there altogether?

Learning objective
(YR) Count on to find out how many more are needed to make a larger number.

You will need
A set of large dominoes; number fans; a screen.

8 How many more?

What to do
- Reveal one half of a domino from behind the screen. Tell the class how many spots the domino has in total.
- Demonstrate how to work out how many spots are on the other side of the domino by counting on from the smaller to the larger number. Raise a finger to represent each of the extra ones counted.
- Ask the children to show their answer with a number fan.

Target questions
- What number do I need to add to 4 to make 8?
- What is 5 count on 2?
- Explain how you worked out the missing number of dots.

Learning objective
(Y1) Use everyday language to describe some features of familiar 3D and 2D shapes.

You will need
A shape or picture of a shape for everyone in the class.

9 Match me

What to do
- Ask the children to stand in a circle to play a game called 'Match me'.
- Give each child a shape. Keep your shape concealed.
- Make a statement such as: *My shape has straight sides and is not a square.* Ask the children who think they could be holding the same shape as you to remain standing. Everyone else must sit down.
- Continue giving clues about the properties of your shape until all children who are holding other shapes have sat down.
- Repeat the activity with different shapes.

Target questions
- Can you see anyone else who has the same shape as you?
- How many sides does your shape have?

Learning objective
(Y1) To understand and use the vocabulary of comparing and ordering numbers.

You will need
A set of 1-10 or 1-20 number cards pegged in order on a washing line.

10 Number detectives

What to do
- Secretly write down a number in the range 1 to 10 or 1 to 20 Invite the children to try and work out the answer by asking questions such as, *Is it more than 5?*
- As the children eliminate numbers, let them remove them from the washing line. Continue until one number remains.
- Reveal your number and praise the children for guessing correctly.
- Increase the challenge by setting a time limit or restricting the number of questions the children are allowed to ask.

Target questions
- Can you peg the numbers back on the number line in order?
- How many of the numbers on the washing line are more than 5?
- Can you explain what the words *more* and *less* mean?

Learning objective
(Y1) Count back in ones from any small number.

You will need
0-30 number cards.

11 Blast off

What to do
- Sit the class together in a circle. Spread the number cards out face down on the floor.
- Ask a child to pick a card and read it out to the child on their left. That child should call out the number that is 1 less.
- Let the count continue back in ones around the circle until someone says zero.
- When zero is reached, shout *BLAST OFF!* together. The child who said zero should 'blast off' and run around the circle and back to their place.
- Encourage the group to anticipate who will blast off each time.

Target questions
- Are the numbers getting bigger or smaller each time?
- If Sam picks 5 and we count back in ones, who will blast off?

Learning objective
(Y1) Give a sensible estimate of a number of objects that can be checked by counting.

You will need
A container with up to 20 pencils; a 0-20 number line; whiteboards or paper and pens.

12 Great estimate

What to do
- Show the children the container of pencils. Ask them to try and make a 'great estimate' of the number of pencils. Explain that a 'great estimate' means guessing close to the actual number.
- Let the children record their estimates.
- Count the objects together. Circle the total on a number line. Ask the children to locate the number they estimated on the number line. Say, that the closer it is to the actual number, the better their estimate.

Target questions
- Did you estimate too many or too few pencils?
- Do you think your estimate was a great estimate? Why?

<table>
<tr><td>

Learning objective
(Y1) Count on and back in twos.

</td></tr>
</table>

You will need
Number cards showing even numbers up to 20; two teddies.

13 Stepping stones

What to do
● Sit in a circle together. Randomly spread the number cards out face up on the floor. Place a teddy on number 20.
● Explain that the numbers represent stepping stones in a crocodile infested lake. The teddy is stranded. The other teddy needs help to rescue him.
● The second teddy needs to go on the stepping stones in the correct order – moving to the number that is 2 more each time.
● Ask different children to move the teddy until he reaches his friend. Then they must help the bears return by counting back in twos.
● Finally arrange the number cards in order.

Target questions
● What could you use to work out which stepping stone teddy needs to move to next?
● Are the numbers getting bigger or smaller each time?

Learning objective
(Y1) Count on or back in steps of one or ten.

You will need
A large 100-square.

14 Stamp on ten

What to do
● Repeat counting on and back in tens starting from ten. Point to each of the ten numbers on the 100-square.
● Explain that you would like everyone to count in ones from 0 to 100. Tell the children that each time they reach a tens number you would like them to stamp hard on the floor as they say it.
● Repeat the activity counting back from 100 to 0. Let the children suggest a different way of marking the tens numbers such as shouting loudly or clapping.

Target questions
● How many stamps did we do altogether?
● If we count on from 24 what will be the first number we stamp on?

Learning objective
(Y1) To use everyday language to describe features of familiar 3D and 2D shapes.

You will need
A 2D or 3D shape for each member of the group.

15 All change

What to do
● Sit in a circle together with each child holding a shape.
● Give an instruction, such as: *Squares all change!* Children holding a square should stand up and move to a different place in the circle.
● Vary the instructions such as: *Shapes with straight sides all change!*
● Let confident children call out an instruction for the rest of the group to follow. This will enable you to assess which children are able to use appropriate vocabulary to describe the properties of shapes.

Target questions
● What is your shape called?
● Describe what your shape looks like.

Learning objective
(Y1) To count on or back in twos.

You will need
A tambourine; a large clear space.

16 Footprints

What to do
● Instruct the children to stand in a space.
● Tell them to imagine that they are playing in the snow.
● Explain that each time you strike the tambourine you would like them to jump forwards in a line.
● Strike the tambourine and then ask the children to say how many footprints they have made in the snow. Tell them to jump again – how many footprints are there now? (Suggest that the children count in twos, counting each pair of their footprints as a 2.)
● Finally, practise counting on in twos on a number line.

Target questions
● If you jump twice how many footprints will you make?
● How many jumps would I have to make to leave 10 footprints?

Learning objective
(Y2) To know by heart addition and subtraction facts for each number to at least 10.

You will need
0-10 number cards per pair of children.

17 Target number

What to do
● Ask the children to work in pairs, each with a set of number cards.
● Write a number in the range of 1 to 10 on the board, such as 7. Tell each pair to pick two number cards that total 7.
● Ask each pair to hold their number cards up to face you. Ask different children to read out their numbers.
● Repeat the activity for other target numbers.
● Repeat the activity, this time splitting the number into three.

Target questions
● How do you know that your two numbers total 7?
● How many ways can you make 7 by adding two numbers?

Learning objective
(Y1) To understand and use the vocabulary of comparing and ordering numbers.

You will need
Ten toy vehicles; ten cardboard stars labelled 1st – 10th (or first to tenth); a piece of string.

18 Order, order!

What to do
● Spread the piece of string on the floor. Arrange the ten vehicles at different distances from it.
● Explain that the vehicles are having a race and that the string is the finishing line.
● Read out one of the stars and invite a child to place it next to the appropriate vehicle.
● Repeat with the rest of the stars and then read them in order.
● Ask the children to close their eyes while you take one of the stars away. Which card has disappeared?
● Pick a child to write what they think it says on the board.

Target questions
● Which vehicle is going to finish first? How do you know?
● What do you notice about the order of the numbers on the stars?

🔲 **15**

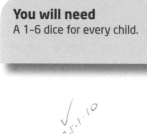

Learning objective
(Y1) To identify doubles and know by heart addition doubles up to 5 + 5.

You will need
A 1–6 dice for every child.

19 Doubles

What to do

● Organise the children to work in pairs. On an agreed signal, tell everyone to roll their dice.
● Tell them to look at the number of spots on each dice, and if it is the same shout *Double!*
● Whenever the children make a double, the first person to shout out how many spots there are altogether scores a point.
● Ask each pair of children to keep a tally of their scores. Keep repeating this until you feel the children have had enough practice.
● Within each pair, the child with the most points at the end of the game is the winner.

Target questions

● What is double 3?
● Can someone explain what the word *double* means?
● Which number makes a total of 10 if you double it?

20 Two hand draw

Learning objective
(Y1) To combine two sets to make a total.

What to do

● Organise the class to work in pairs. On an agreed signal, tell everyone to pull one hand from behind their back, holding up some fingers.
● Tell each pair to calculate how many fingers they are holding up altogether by either counting all of the fingers or by counting on from the number of fingers on one hand.
● Make the activity more challenging by asking the children to use both hands (and hold up to ten fingers up).

Target questions

● How did you work out how many fingers you and your partner were holding up altogether?
● If 4 + 3 = 7, what is 3 + 4?
● Do you think it is more sensible to count on from the smaller or the larger number? Why?

 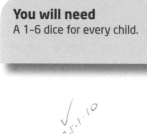

21 Number spotter

Learning objective
(YR) Estimate a number in the range that can be counted reliably, then check by counting.

You will need
Number fans; collections of interesting objects; a cloth.

What to do
● Place a set of up to six objects, such as shells, on the floor.
● Give the group a few seconds to look at the set of objects and then cover it up with the cloth.
● Ask the children to show how many objects they think are in the set by holding up the corresponding number on their number fan.
● Choose a child to count the objects.
● Repeat using different sets of objects.

Target questions
● What did you do to make sure you counted every shell?
● Do you think there are more or less than five shells?

22 Outdoor counting

Learning objective
(Y1) Count reliably at least 20 objects.

You will need
An outdoor area; a small plastic tray per child.

What to do
● Give each child a plastic tray. Call out a number. Tell the class that they have one minute to go and collect that many objects in their tray.
● Instruct the children to swap trays with a partner and count the objects in their partner's tray to check the accuracy of their counting.
● Discuss ways of organising counting to make it easier to count accurately (such as arranging the objects in a line).

Target questions
● How can you be sure that you have counted all the leaves?
● Can you check a different way?

23 Number swap shop

Learning objective
(Y1) Know what each digit in a two-digit number represents.

You will need
A set of number cards (selected according to the ability of your class).

What to do
● Organise the class so that they are standing in a circle with one child in the middle. Give each of the children in the circle a number card and ask them to place it on the floor in front of them, face-up.
● Give an instruction to the child in the middle, such as: *Swap places with number 75/a number which has two tens.* And so on.
● From time to time give an instruction for the whole group to follow, such as: *All the numbers with three tens swap places.*
● Make the activity competitive by having two children in the middle. The two children have to race to be the first to locate the number.

Target questions
● What does the 2 in 32 stand for?
● How many tens and ones are there in this number?

24 Five little ducks

What to do
● Sing 'Five little ducks went swimming one day'. Pick five children to stand at the front and pretend to be the ducks.
● Hold up five yellow cubes to represent the ducks. Hide some of the cubes behind your back. Ask: *How many ducks have swum away?* Demonstrate how to do this by counting on from the number of ducks that can be seen, up to the number 5.
● Split the children into pairs and give each pair a set of five yellow cubes. Ask them to take it in turns to hide some of the cubes behind their back. Can their partner work out how many ducks have swum away?
● Repeat the activity at a later date using a different number of cubes.

Target questions
● There are 5 ducks. If 2 swim away how many will be left?
● How did you work out how many cubes were behind my back?

25 Grabbing gloves

What to do
● Choose a child to put on the 'grabbing' gloves and try to grab as many of the objects as they can in one go.
● Ask the child to count how many objects they grabbed. With the class, discuss different strategies to keep track of where the count begins and ends.
● Give each child a chance to wear the 'grabbing' gloves. Keep a score chart. At the end of the activity compare the scores to see who grabbed the most.

Target questions
● How could you arrange the objects to make sure you do not count any of them twice?
● Can you count the objects without touching them?

26 Who is the greatest?

What to do
- Choose two children to stand at the front of the class. Give them each a number card to hold.
- Tell the children that you are going to play a game called 'Who is the greatest?'. Explain that 'greatest' is another word which can be used to describe the largest number in a set.
- Ask the children to show their cards and ask the class: *Who is the greatest?* Encourage the class to chant the answer together. Let the child holding the greatest number stay at the front and invite a different opponent to come to the front.
- Make the game more challenging by comparing a set of three or more numbers.

Target questions
- How do you know that one number is greater than the other?
- What method did you use to work out which number was the greatest?

27 Hot potato (1)

What to do
- Ask the children to sit in a circle. Tell the children the ball is a 'hot potato' – if they hold it for too long they will get burned. Roll the ball across the circle and shout out *One!*
- Tell the child who receives the ball to roll it on to a different child as quickly as they can, shouting *Two!* as they release the ball. Continue in this manner.
- After a while shout: *Switch!* Tell the children to switch to counting backwards. Shout: *Switch!* several times during the activity.

Target questions
- What number comes after 5?
- Are the numbers getting bigger or smaller?
- What happens to the number sequence when I say *Switch*?

<table>
<tr><td>

Learning objective
(Y1) To say the number
that is 10 more or less
than any given number.

</td></tr>
</table>

You will need
A small ball.

28 Hot potato (2)

What to do
● Ask the children to sit in a circle. Roll the 'hot potato' to each child in turn. As you roll the ball, call out a number.
● Tell the child with the ball to roll it back quickly. Ask them to call out the number that is ten more than your number as they release the ball.
● Repeat the activity, but this time ask the children to call out the number that is ten less than your number.

Target questions
● What is 10 more than 51?
● When we add 10 to a number, what happens to the digit in the tens column/units column?

Learning objective
(Y1/2) To know what each digit in a two-digit number represents.

You will need
Sets of place value cards; 10p and 1p coins.

29 Match my digits

What to do
● Organise the class to work in pairs. Give each pair a set of place value cards and ask them to make a two-digit number.
● Make a two-digit number yourself.
● Explain that if a pair has made a number with the same number of tens/ones as your number they will win 10p/1p accordingly.
● Hold up your number. Ask: *What is my number? How many tens/ones does my number have?* Award ten pence and one pence coins to those children who have matched a digit in your number.
● At the end of the activity the pair with the most money are the winners.

Target questions
● What does the four in 24 stand for?
● Which digit tells you how many tens there are in this number?

Learning objective
(Y2) To know by heart
facts for the two and ten
multiplication tables.

You will need
Ten 10p or 2p coins for each child.

30 Times tables

What to do
● Explain that today you are going to practise number facts for the two-times table.
● Give each child in the group a set of ten 2p coins. Write the multiples of 2 to 20 on the board.
● Say, for example: *5 × 2.* Show how to work out the answer using five 2p coins and counting *2, 4, 6, 8, 10.*
● Encourage the children to work out other questions using their coins.
● Repeat the activity for the ten-times table by giving the children 10p coins.

Target questions
● What is 5 × 10?
● Is 31 in the ten-times table? How do you know?

Learning objective
(Y1) To understand and use the vocabulary of comparing and ordering numbers.

You will need
Number cards 1-10; a whiteboard and pen.

31 Order or bust!

What to do
- Draw five boxes in a line on the board. Tell the class that you are going to turn over the number cards, one at a time, and they must choose which box to write the number in.
- The aim of the game is to enter five digits in order from smallest to largest.
- Turn over a number. Ask: *Where shall I write this number? Why?*
- Continue until all the boxes are filled in or until you go 'bust' (you go bust if you turn over a number that cannot be entered into any of the remaining empty boxes).
- Discuss the tactics of the game. Play again.

Target questions
- Would it be sensible to put number one in this box?
- Why did we go bust?

Learning objective
(YR) Work out by counting how many more are needed to make a larger number.

You will need
A cardboard star; a large 1–6 dice; individual whiteboards/paper and pens.

32 Star number

What to do
- Write six consecutive numbers on the board.
- Write down the number that is 6 more than the largest number on the star.
- Explain that the object of the game is to make the 'star number'.
- Instruct the class to choose one of the numbers on the board and write it down. Roll the dice. Tell the children to add the number of spots shown on the dice onto the number on their board.
- Any children who have made the star number score a point.

Target questions
- What number do I need to roll to get to the star number from ten?
- What method did you use to add the numbers together?

Learning objective
(Y1/2) To describe and extend simple number sequences.

You will need
Rewards such as stickers; a small whiteboard and pen between two.

33 Code breaker

What to do
- Give the children in pairs, a whiteboard and pen.
- Write a sequence of numbers on the board, such as: 4, 5, 6, 7, _ ; 64, 54, 44, 34, _. Explain that the numbers are part of a secret code and if the children crack the code they could win a prize.
- Ask the children, in their pairs, to look carefully at the numbers. Can they crack the code and work out the next number in the sequence?
- Ask one pair to describe the number sequence and explain how they cracked the code. Reward them with a sticker.

Target questions
- Are the numbers getting smaller or larger?
- Circle the numbers on the number line. Can you continue the pattern?

34 Hands and feet

What to do
- Sit in a circle. Ask one child to put both their feet into the circle. Instruct the next child to put their feet into the circle. How many feet are in the circle now?
- Continue around the circle counting in twos until everyone has both feet in the circle.
- Then count back to zero in twos as everyone, in turn, takes their feet back out of the circle.
- Next, tell each child to put in their hands (either both or just one hand) to practise counting in tens or fives - by counting the number of fingers in the circle.

Target questions
- Who will say 12?
- How many twos did we count?

Learning objectives
(Y1) Describe and extend number sequences.
Count on or back in steps of 2, 5 or 10.

35 Lucky lottery

What to do
- Write the numbers 0 to 20 randomly on the board. Give each child a lottery ticket.
- Tell everyone to choose five numbers from the selection on the board and write them in the five boxes on their lottery ticket.
- Draw numbers from the bag and call them out. Whenever you say a number that a child has on their lottery ticket they should cross it out. The first player to cross out all their numbers and shout *JACKPOT!* wins.

Target questions
- Can you see this number on your ticket?
- Count along the number line until you reach 15. Have you got the number 15 on your lottery ticket?

Learning objective
(Y1) To read numbers from 0 to at least 20.

You will need
A pretend lottery ticket for each child (a small piece of paper divided into five sections will do); a set of 0-20 digit cards in a bag; stickers (or other small rewards).

36 It's a rollover

What to do
- Write all the even numbers to 20 on the board. Give each child a 'lottery ticket' and tell them to choose five numbers from the selection on the board and write them in the five boxes on their lottery ticket.
- Play the game in the same way as 'Lucky lottery' (above), but this time ask children to cross out the number that is double the number you draw out of the bag.

Target questions
- Find a domino which is double 5. How many spots does it have altogether?
- What number would I need to draw out of the bag so that you could cover the number 12 on your board? Explain how you know.

Learning objective
(Y1) To recall addition doubles to 10 + 10.

You will need
A 'lucky lottery' ticket for each child (see, 'Lucky lottery', above); a set of digit cards 1-10 in a bag; stickers or other small rewards.

<table>
<tr><td>

Learning objective
(Y1) To add or subtract a small number by counting on or back in ones.

You will need
A plastic box; a small beanbag; a dice numbered 1, 1, 2, 2, 3, 3; a bucket.

</td><td>

37 In the bucket

What to do
● Stand in a circle around the bucket. In turn, give each child the beanbag. Ask them to throw it into the bucket. If it goes in, roll the dice to determine the number of points they score. Record their score.
● Each time the beanbag goes in, roll the dice and add the number to the score. Write the new total on the board.
● Repeat the activity the next day. Can the children beat their score?
● Alternatively, focus on subtraction. Start with 20 points. Subtract the number on the dice each time. Can the children get back to zero?

Target questions
● Can you count how many times the beanbag goes in the bucket?
● Put your finger on number 3 on the number line. Jump on 2 more. What is the score now?

</td></tr>
</table>

38 Penalty shoot out

Learning objective
(Y1) To recognise odd and even numbers.

You will need
A bag containing a set of 0-30 football shaped number cards.

What to do
● Split the class into two teams - 'The Odds' and 'The Evens'.
● Draw two goals posts on the board, label them Odd and Even. Explain that you are going to play a game called 'Penalty shoot out'. The first team to score 5 goals will be the winners.
● Nominate a player to take a penalty. Both players take a football card from the bag. If the 'Even team' select an even number they score (stick the number in the even goal). If they pick an odd number they miss (stick the number outside the goal). Continue in this way.
● Act as the referee and intervene if children are unsure whether a number is odd or even.

Target questions
● Is 6 an odd or even number?
● How can we check if a number is odd or even?

39 King/Queen of the castle

Learning objective
(Y1) To compare two given numbers and say which is more or less.

You will need
A shuffled set of 1-20 cards (put half of the cards in a special bag); a cardboard crown.

What to do
● Ask the children to sit in a circle. Spread half of the number cards face down on the floor.
● Choose a child to wear the crown and sit on a chair.
● Tell the King or Queen to take a number from their special bag and hold it up. Invite a child to turn over one of the number cards on the floor. If their number is larger, they become the new King or Queen of the castle.

Target questions
● Which is the largest number - 5 or 7?
● How could we check using this number line?

◻ 23

Learning objective
(Y1) To understand and use the vocabulary of comparing and ordering ordinal numbers.

You will need
Small whiteboards or paper and pens (one between two); word cards.

40 What's my word?

What to do
- Think of a word (such as, *yellow*). Tell the class how many letters there are in your word.
- Ask the children, in pairs, to draw a dash to represent each letter.
- Disclose the letters in the word, one by one. Use ordinal numbers to describe the position of each letter.
- Ask the children to hold up their boards. Check to see who has followed the instructions correctly.
- Let the children play 'What's my word?' in pairs. Prepare a set of word cards for the children to select from.

Target questions
- What is the first letter of the word?
- Can you tell me the position of the letter *e* in this word?

Learning objective
(Y2) To count on or back in ones from a two-digit number.

You will need
A hat; sticky labels with different two-digit numbers written on them; a large 1–6 dice.

41 Counting hat

What to do
- Show the class the counting hat. Stick the number 25 on the hat. Say that the hat helps you to add or subtract a small number to 25. Ask a child to roll the dice to determine what this number will be.
- Put on the hat, and at the same time say *25*. Then count on 3, modelling how to use your fingers as a tally.
- Repeat the activity, changing the number on the hat each time.
- Let different children use the counting hat. Encourage the rest of the group to put on an imaginary hat as they say the starting number.

Target questions
- Put on the counting hat. Count on 1. What is your answer?
- What can we use to check our answers?

Learning objective
(YR) To partition a given number of objects into two groups.

You will need
A small box (draw teeth and eyes on the top of the box and write NUMBER CRUNCHER on the side); interlocking cubes; individual whiteboards (or sheets of paper) and pens.

42 Number cruncher

What to do
- Put a tower of 7 cubes into the Number Cruncher. Say that the Number Cruncher will crunch the tower into two smaller pieces.
- Ask: *What might the cube tower look like when it comes out of the 'cruncher'?* (For example, a tower of 4 and a tower of 3 cubes.) Working in pairs, ask the children to record their answers.
- While the children record their guesses, break the tower into two pieces. Show the children the two towers.
- Repeat the activity with different cube towers.

Target questions
- How many different ways can you break this tower of seven cubes into two pieces?
- How do you know that 5 + 2 = 7?

Learning objective
(Y1) To compare two familiar numbers and give a number which lies between them.

You will need
0-30 number cards.

43 Number sandwich

What to do
● Give everyone in the class a number card to hold.
● Choose two children to look at the numbers they are holding and discuss which is the largest/smallest? Explain that these two numbers represent the bread in a number sandwich.
● Ask the class to put their hand up if they are holding a number that lies between these two numbers. Pick one of these children to be the sandwich filling and stand between the two 'pieces of bread'.
● Repeat the activity, choosing different children each time. Make sandwiches with more than one filling.

Target questions
● Which number is bigger – 5 or 10?
● What numbers lie between 5 and 10?

Learning objective
(Y1) To read, write and order numbers to at least 20.

You will need
Individual whiteboards (or paper) and pens; number cards 0-20.

44 What's my number?

What to do
● Number all the children, 'one' or 'two'. Give all the 'ones' a whiteboard and a pen and tell them to stand in a space.
● Give each of the 'twos' a number card. Tell them to go and trace the number onto a number one's back with their finger.
● Challenge the number ones to write the number they think they felt.
● Ask the children to turn the boards and number cards to face you so that you can see who answered correctly.

Target questions
● Can you think of a number that is written using just straight lines?
● Is the number on your board a one digit or a two-digit number?

Learning objective
(YR) To order a set of familiar numbers.

You will need
Large 0-30 number cards; a number line.

45 All in a line

What to do
● Give five children a number card. Tell them to ask each other, *What is your number?*
● When you say: *Order, order!* they must line up in ascending order.
● Ask these children to call out their numbers in the order that they are stood. Choose a child to point to each of the numbers on a number line.
● If the numbers appear on the number line in the same order that the children are standing, the task has been completed successfully.
● Repeat the activity using different sets of numbers, by giving out more cards or by asking the children to line up in descending order.

Target questions
● Which is the largest/smallest number?
● How do you know that 13 is bigger than 10?

■ 25

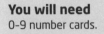

Learning objective
(Y1/2) To know what each
digit in a two-digit number
represents.

You will need
0–9 number cards.

46 Ring, ring!

What to do
● Use the number cards to make a six-digit telephone number on the
board, such as 553461.
● Ask the children to suggest different two-digit numbers that can be
made using these six digits. List the numbers on the board.
● Tell the children that you would like them to rub off the two-digit
numbers on the board, one at a time.
● Give a range of instructions, such as: *Rub out the number which has
three tens and six ones* or *rub out the smallest number.*
● Continue until there are no numbers left on the board.

Target questions
● What does the 1 in 17 mean?
● How many other numbers can you see with one ten?

Learning objective
(Y1) To know by heart all
pairs of numbers with a
total 10.

You will need
Two sets of 0–10 number
cards shuffled together.

47 Bowled over

What to do
● Split the class in half with the two groups standing facing each other.
Tell the children that they are going to play an imaginary game of
cricket. Toss a coin to decide which group will be the batters/bowlers.
● Show the bowlers a number card and explain that you would like
them to 'bowl' that number to the batters (shouting the number out
aloud at the same time). The batters must then 'hit' the number that
makes it up to ten.
● Swap the two groups over after every six balls.

Target questions
● What number do I have to add to 4 to make 10?
● Can you tell me all the pairs of numbers that make 10?

Learning objective
(Y1) To count reliably at
least 20 objects.

You will need
Several 1–6 dice; 1–20
number tracks; different
coloured counters.

48 Knock it off

What to do
● Play this game in groups of three or four, or two class teams.
● Take it in turns to shake three dice, count the total number of spots
on the dice and cover that number on the number track with a counter.
If there is already a counter on that number, a player can 'knock it off'
and replace it with one their own.
● The winner is the first player to cover five numbers.

Target questions
● Why do we have to start from number 1 each time we count?
● When you count the spots, which number tells you how many spots
there are altogether?

49 Number king

What to do

- Choose a child to be the number king/queen and wear the crown.
- Write a number from 0 to 20 on a Post-it Note. Stick it on the front of the crown without the king or queen seeing it.
- Tell the 'royal servants' to look at the number. Ask them to hold up the number partner to make 20 on their number fan.
- The number king must use this information to deduce what number is on the crown. When they answer correctly they may choose the next king/queen.
- Record each pair of numbers on the board and revise them at the end of the game.

Target questions

- If we know that 3 and 7 makes 10, what do we have to add to three to make 20?
- Can you tell me all the pairs of numbers that make 20?

Learning objective
(Y2) To know all pairs of numbers with a total of twenty.

You will need
0-20 number cards or number fans for everyone in the group; a cardboard crown; small Post-it Notes.

50 Eyes closed

What to do

- Ask the class to close their eyes and imagine that they are standing on the number four on a 100-square. Say: *Move to the number that is ten more than four. What number are you standing on now?*
- Tell the children to 'stand' on other numbers and then add or subtract ten or one.
- Ask different children to describe the 'quick tricks' they can use for adding or subtracting 10 or 1 on a 100-square. (See 'Swim to shore' on page 38.)

Target questions

- Imagine that you are standing on the number 5 on a number line. Move to the number that is 1 more than 5. What number are you on now?
- 61, 71, 81 - what is the next number in the sequence?

Learning objective
(Y1) To say the number that is 1 or 10 more or less than any given number.

You will need
A 100-square.

Dotty the dog

Learning objectives
(Y1) Know the number names and recite them in order to at least 20 from and back to 0.
(Y1) Count reliably at least 20 objects.

Mental starter
See the starter 1 on page 10.

You will need
Photocopiable page 29 per child in the less able group, plus one A3 copy; a big pot of counters; four 1-6 dice.

Whole class work
● Ask the class to sit in a circle and count as you put some counters onto the enlarged photocopiable. Ask: *How many dots are on Dotty the dog altogether? How do you know? How can we count them?*
● Repeat for different amounts of dots in the range 1 to 20 and ask the children how they know the answer.

Group work
● Give each child a copy of photocopiable page 29. Tell them to put 20 counters onto their dog. Ask the children to check that the child sitting to their left has correctly placed 20 counters on the dog.
● Explain that the children are going to play a game with the object being to have the 'dottiest' dog. Ask the children: *How will you know who is the winner?*
● Establish that it will be necessary to count up and compare the number of counters on each dog to find out who has the most.
● Ask the children to sit in a circle. The first player must roll the dice, remove the corresponding number of counters from their dog and place them on the dog of the player to their right. That person then rolls the dice and continues in the same way.
● Play continues until everyone in the circle has had two turns. For extra counting practice, stop play at intervals and ask different children to count up the number of dots on their dog.
● At the end of the game, ask each child to count aloud the number of dots on their dog. Record the scores on the board to see who has the dottiest dog!

Paired work
● Divide the children into pairs to play again. Work alongside children who have difficulty counting accurately. Ask them to count up the spots on their dog after each turn. Suggest strategies such as touching each counter or arranging the counters in lines.

Plenary
● Give each child a handful of counters. Ask them to arrange them on their dog, count them and then tell you how many counters they each have. Ask: *How can you make sure that you count all the spots? Can you check in a different way?*

Potential difficulties	Further support
Unable to count the counters in a random arrangement.	Organise the counters in a linear arrangement.
Children are not aware that the last number in the count is the total number.	Model counting all the counters then ask: *How many do I have?*

Moving on
● Start the game with 30 counters each to give children experience of counting sets of objects to beyond 30.

Dotty the dog

One more Max

Learning objectives
(Y1) Count on and back in ones from any small number.
(Y1) Within the range 0 to 30 say the number that is one more or less than any given number.

Mental starter
See the starter 5 on page 11.

You will need
A laminated copy of photocopiable page 31 per pair of children plus an enlarged copy for Group work; number fans; counters; a 1–30 number line.

Whole class work
● Write a number on the board such as 15. Tell the children, in pairs, to hold up the number that is one more on their number fan.

Group work
● Hold up the enlarged photocopiable. Explain that 'One more Max' is a little boy who is never satisfied and always wants one more.
● Ask the group to pretend they are Max and hold one finger up and say: *I want one more!*
● Tell the group a simple number story about Max. Choose different children to act the parts of Mum and Max. Place the photocopiable with a pile of counters near by.
● Say: *Max's Mum gave him 10 sweets.* (Ask Mum to count 10 counters into Max's bag and write the number 10 in the box on the handle of the bag.) *Of course Max didn't say thank you to his mum. Can you guess what he said?* (Tell Max to repeat the phrase *I want one more* with the accompanying action.) *So his mum gave him one more sweet.* (Place 1 more counter in Max's bag to represent this.)
● Ask: *Is the number on the bag still correct? Why not? What should it say now?* Say together: *1 more than 10 is 11* while pointing to the numbers on the number line.
● Tell other simple stories about Max which involve adding 1 more to numbers in the range 0 to 30.

Paired work
● Give each pair of children a copy of photocopiable page 31 and some counters. Ask them to take it in turns to make up their own 'one more than' number stories for their partner to solve using the counters.

Plenary
● Sit in a circle with the less able group. Play a variation of the hot potato game (see the mental starter on page 11). Call out a number and, at the same time, roll the ball. The child who receives the ball should call out the number that is 'one more'.

Potential difficulties	Further support
Children have difficulty adding 1 more.	Demonstrate how to add 1 more on a number line by moving on to the next number.
Children are not able to count on from a number.	Practise counting on in ones from different numbers during Mental starters.

Moving on
● Challenge the children to add '1 more' to larger numbers using a 100-square for reference.
● Introduce the concept of 'one less than' using the character 'One less Lucy'- a little girl who always 'loses one'!

One more Max

One more, one less

Learning objectives
(Y1) Count on and back in ones from any small number.
(Y1) Within the range 0 to 30 say the number that is one more or less than any given number.

Mental starter
See the starter 27 on page 19.

You will need
Photocopiable page 33 (cut out several copies of the spinner from thin card); sets of 0-20 number cards; a washing line and pegs; paper plates; a bag of dried beans or pasta shapes.

Whole class work
- Shuffle a set of 0-20 number cards and deal them out. Instruct the child holding the number ten to peg it in the middle of the washing line.
- Spin the spinner and ask: *Can the person who has the number which is 1 more than or 1 less than 10 come and peg it on the line?* Continue until all the cards have been pegged up in numerical order.
- Count along and back the number line together.

Group work
- Show the group the 1 more/less vocabulary cards. Ask them to explain what is happening in each of the pictures. Display the pictures on the board so that the group can refer to them throughout the lesson.
- Ask the children in the group to count ten beans onto a plate. Spin the spinner. Show the children how to adjust the number of beans on their plate according to the operation shown.
- Play a game called 'Dinner time'. Give each child a paper plate with ten beans on it and a spinner. Tell the children to spin the spinner and add or take a bean from their plate. Tell them to keep repeating this (for about five minutes) until you shout *Dinner time!*
- The player with the most beans on their plate is the winner.

Paired work
- Ask the children to repeat the game with a partner. Encourage the use of key vocabulary.

Plenary
- Ask the group to explain what you have to do to find the number that is 1 more or less than a number. Discuss how a number line can help us to find the answers more quickly.
- Write a number from 0 to 20 on the board. Spin the spinner. Ask the group to shout out the number which is 1 more/less as quickly as they can. Repeat for other numbers.

Potential difficulties	Further support
Children are unable to say which number is 1 more/one less than a number.	Display a number line for children to refer to.
Children confuse the operations of one more than and 1 less than.	Remind the children to look at the picture cards if they are unsure whether to add or take a bean from the plate.

Moving on
- Modify the group activity – place two numbers on the table at the beginning of the game, such as 5 and 11. This will give the children more options to consider when it is their turn to lay a card.
- Repeat the activities with larger numbers.

One more, one less

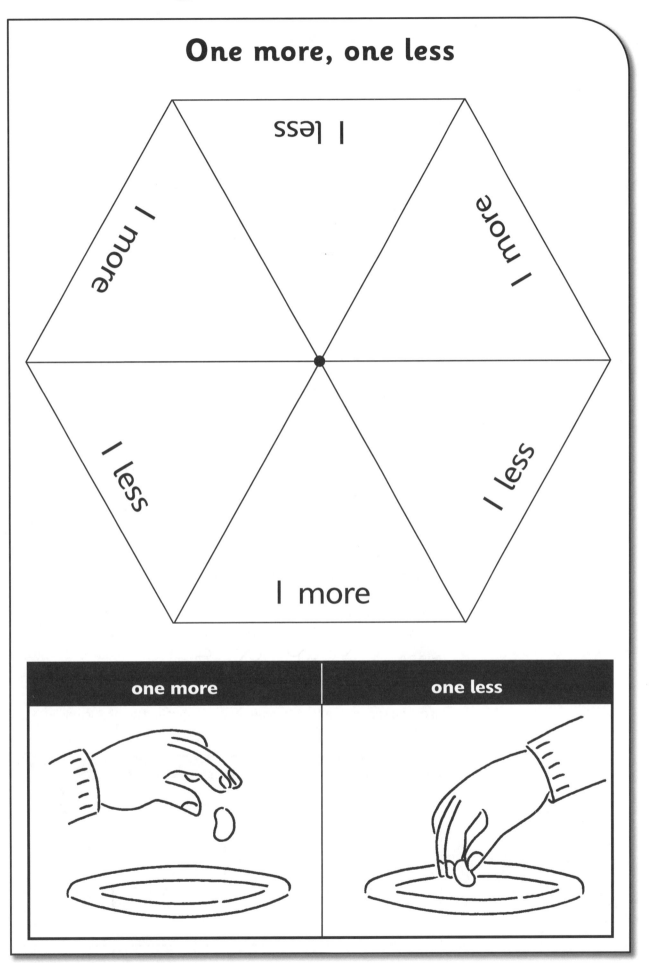

one more	one less

Race to 100

Learning objective
(Y1) Count in tens from and back to 0.

Mental starter
See the Mental starter, '2 - Money Box' on page 10.

You will need
Photocopiable page 35 between each pair of children; a 100-square; a counting stick; a toy car; a set of number cards for every child; counters; several 1-6 dice; blank 10-space number tracks for every child.

Whole class work

• Count along the counting stick and back in multiples of 10. Show the children how to 'explode' 10 fingers to represent each 10 counted.
• Tell the children to count in tens in their heads as you point to each division on the counting stick. Stop at different points, ask: *What number have I reached? What will the next number be?*

Group work

• Spread a set of number cards out face-up on the floor for the less able learners. Work together to order the multiples of 10 in ascending order.
• Encourage the children to notice the pattern of 1, 2, 3, 4 within the numbers.
• Place the car on number 10. Let each child have a turn to drive the toy car along the constructed number line and back, saying the numbers out loud as the car passes over them.
• Turn the number cards face down. Ask the children: *Can you drive the car onto number 30. How did you know which number it was? What will the next number be?*

Paired work

• Give each pair of children a 'Race to 100' game board, two blank number tracks, two counters and a 1-6 dice. Explain the instructions:
1. Each child should take it in turns to shake the dice and move their counters the corresponding number of spaces around the track, in either direction. The aim of the game is to land on all the multiples of 10 to 100 in ascending order; they should aim for a 10 on their first go.
2. Explain that when their counter lands on 10 they should write the number 10 in the first space on their blank number track. They should then try to land on 20 and so on. The winner is the first child to fill in their blank number track to 100.
3. Repeat the game, filling in the numbers in descending order.

Plenary

• Revise multiples of 10 with the less able group by asking the children to play the 'Tens Race' in pairs. The children should race their partner to see who can be the first to order a set of shuffled number cards in either ascending or descending order.

Potential difficulties	Further support
Children are unable to order multiples of 10 correctly.	Display a 100-square for reference. Highlight the tens column.
Children find it difficult to work out the next number in the tens sequence.	Demonstrate how to chant the multiples of 10 from 0 to work out the next number of tens.

Moving On
• Play a more challenging version of the game. Allow children to collect the multiples of 10 in any order but still placing them in the correct order on the track.

Race to 100

Start

Ten more machine

Learning objective
(Y1) Within the range 0 to 30 say the number that is 10 more or less than any given number.

Mental starter
See the starter 10 on page 14.

You will need
Photocopiable page 37; a 100-square for each child in the less able group; number cards (1-20); a large 100-square; coloured crayons or pens; Multilink cubes.

Whole class work

● Display the large 100-square on the board. Select a coloured crayon and circle the number 1. Ask a child to start at the number 1, count on 10 more and circle the number they land on in the same colour. Say: *1 and 10 more makes 11.* Repeat this process for other numbers in the range 0 to 10. Use a different colour to circle each pair of numbers.
● Encourage children to notice that each time you count on 10 from the first number, you land on the number directly below this number. Highlight that the number of units in a number does not change when a 10 is added.

Group work

● Write the numbers 1 to 10 down one side of the board and the numbers 11 to 20 randomly down the other side.
● Demonstrate how the 'ten more' machine works. Place a stick of 10 Multilink cubes on '10 more'. Place 2 cubes on 'Start' at the top of the machine. Push the 2 cubes through the machine in the direction shown by the arrows. Push all of the cubes out of the machine and count the total number of cubes. Say: *2 and 10 more makes 12.* Join up these two numbers on board.
● Let all the children in the group have a turn to work the machine and match a pair of numbers on the board.

Independent work

● Deal each child in the group a number card and ask them to circle the number on their own 100-square. Instruct the children to use their 'ten more' machine to add 10 to the number (using cubes) and then circle the total on their 100-square.
● Encourage children to add 10 to as many numbers as they can. Ask them to notice and describe the pattern which emerges.

Plenary

Ask questions such as: *Can you tell me which number is 10 more than 5 without counting? How did you know? Tell me the number that is 10 more than 15, 25, 35 and so on. What do you notice about all the numbers in this column?*
● Remember to encourage struggling children to answer these questions and provide support.

Potential difficulties	Further support
Children are unable to count on in tens from any small number.	Regularly chant down the columns of a 100-square.
	Encourage the children to count in tens with their eyes closed, visualising the numbers in their head.

Moving On
● Make a 'Ten less' machine to investigate subtracting 10 from a teen number.
● Ask children to use their knowledge of place value to mentally add or subtract 10 from a two-digit number.

Ten more machine

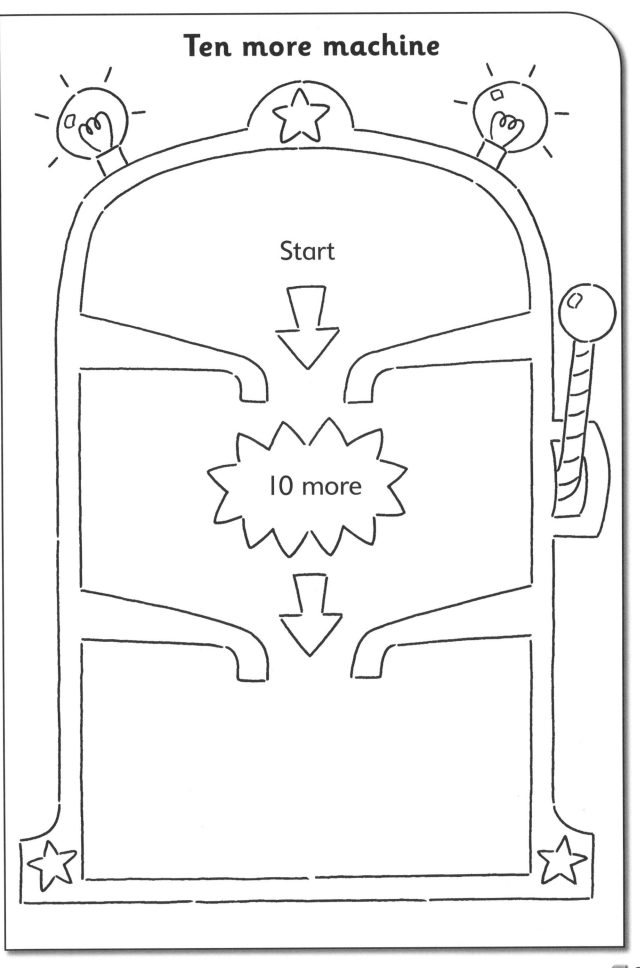

Swim to shore

Whole class work
● Count on and back in tens and ones from different starting points on a 100-square.
● Discuss what happens to the digits in a two-digit number when you count on or back from a number in tens or ones.

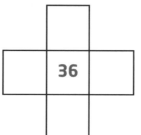

● Draw five boxes on the board (see left) and insert a number in the centre box. Tell the children that it is a section of a 100-square and you would like them to help you fill in the missing numbers.
● Point to the top box. Ask the children to tell you the number that should be in the box and to explain how they know this. Fill in the other missing numbers in turn.

Group work
● Show the group the enlarged copy of 'Swim to Shore'. Fix a counter on number 45 using Blu-Tack. Explain that the counter shows the location of a diver who has been stranded in shark-infested waters! The diver needs to get back to shore as quickly as possible to avoid being eaten.
● Ask a child to spin the spinner, move the counter and call out the diver's new location. For example, for *+10* the counter should be moved to 55. Let the children in the group take it in turns to spin the spinner and move the counter until the diver is safely back on the shore.

Paired work
● Divide the less able children into pairs to play the game. Explain that the winner is the first player to get back to the shore.
● Supervise the children to ensure that they play the game correctly and to enable you to assess their understanding of adding/subtracting ten or one using a 100-square.

Plenary
● Ask different children to explain what happens to the digits in a two-digit number when you count on or back in tens and on or back in ones.
● Stick a blank 100-square on the board. Write 45 in the correct space. Target specific children. Ask them to spin the spinner and then write the correct number in the space on the 100-square.

Potential difficulties	Further support
Children are confused by the number of different operations required to play the game.	Draw arrows on the game board to help children remember the rule for adding and subtracting ten or one on a 100-square.

Name _____

Swim to shore

Shore

1	2	3	4	5	6	7	8	9	10
11	12	13	14	15	16	17	18	19	20
21	22	23	24	25	26	27	28	29	30
31	32	33	34	35	36	37	38	39	40
41	42	43	44	45	46	47	48	49	50
51	52	53	54	55	56	57	58	59	60
61	62	63	64	65	66	67	68	69	70
71	72	73	74	75	76	77	78	79	80
81	82	83	84	85	86	87	88	89	90
91	92	93	94	95	96	97	98	99	100

Shore

Shore

Shore

Mrs Odd and Mr Even

Learning objectives
(Y1) Count on in twos from 0, then 1, and begin to recognise odd or even numbers to about 20 as 'every other number'.
(Y1) Describe and extend number sequences.

Mental starter
See the starter 13 on page 14.

You will need
Photocopiable page 41 (a laminated copy per pair of children); a set of 1–20 number cards per pair of children.

Whole class work
● Pick two children to be Mrs Odd and Mr Even. Give Mrs Odd and Mr Even the appropriate bags to hold. Describe how the two characters keep special numbers inside their bags – Mr Even calls his even numbers and Mrs Odd calls hers odd numbers.
● Introduce Mr Even as a kind man who always shares fairly. Take a number from Mr Even's bag. Tell the children that for example, 4 is an even number because it can be split equally. Demonstrate this visually by giving Mr Even 4 cubes and asking him to share them fairly with you. Repeat this with the rest of his numbers.
● Now turn to Mrs Odd. Say that Mrs Odd is greedy and likes odd numbers because they cannot be split fairly. Pick a number from the bag and show what happens when you try to share an odd number of cubes between two people. There is always one left over, which Mrs Odd likes to keep for herself! Repeat for the other numbers in the bag.

Group work
● Repeat the whole class activity with the group of less able learners.
● Pick two children to be Mrs Odd and Mr Even. Ask the children in the group to describe what they know about the two different characters.

Paired work
● Give each pair of children a laminated copy of 'Mrs Odd and Mr Even', 20 cubes and a set of 1–20 number cards placed face down.
● Instruct the children to turn over the number cards one at a time and use the cubes to work out whether the number is odd or even. Suggest that they do this by counting out the number of cubes and trying to split them equally between themselves and their partner.
● Ask them to write the even numbers in Mr Even's bag and the odd numbers in Mrs Odd's bag. Check the children's answers.

Plenary
● Call out numbers from the 0 to 20 number range and ask different children from the less able group to say whether the numbers are odd or even. Record this by writing an 'O' or 'E' above each number on the number track.
● Ask the children to describe the alternate pattern of odd and even numbers.

Potential difficulties	Further support
Children have difficulty reading numbers 11 to 19.	Have number lines available so that children can count on from 1 to identify an unknown number.

Moving On
● Ask children to investigate the pattern of odd and even numbers from 20 to 30.
● Hold up a number. Challenge the children to shout out *Odd* or *Even*.

Mrs Odd and Mr Even

Mr Even

Even numbers

Mrs Odd

Odd numbers

Pop to the shop

Learning objectives
(Y1) Count on in twos.
(Y1) Describe and extend number sequences.

Mental starter
See the starter 16 on page 15.

You will need
A copy of photocopiable page 43 and a pot of 2p coins per pair of children; a dice labelled 1, 1, 1, 2, 2, 3; counters; a large blank number track; a pair of shoes.

Whole class work
● Place a pair of shoes in front of the group. Explain that a pair consists of two objects. Write the number two in the first space on the blank number track.
● Choose a child to place their shoes behind the first pair. Write the number 4 in the next space on the number track. Continue in this way until you have a row of 10 pairs of shoes and a number track showing all the even numbers from 2 to 20.
● Count along the number track and back with the children.

Paired work
● Divide the less able group into pairs to play 'Pop to the shop' using laminated copies of photocopiable page 43. One player is the 'customer' and the other player is a 'bank clerk'. Give the bank clerk a pot of 2p coins and the customer one 2p coin. Model how to play the game:
1. The customer rolls the dice and moves a counter the correct number of spaces.
2. The bank clerk gives the customer 2p or takes 2p away from the customer according to the instructions given on the space the customer lands on.
3. The customer continues moving around the board until they reach the shop. The customer then counts up the total amount of money they have collected by counting in twos.
4. The customer chooses an item they can afford to buy and counts out the correct number of 2p coins and then colours in the item they have bought.
5. The children swap roles and continue playing until all of the items in the shop have been bought.
● As the children play, assess their ability to count in twos by observing them count up their money. Ask: *Have you got enough money to buy the banana? How many more 2p coins do you need?*

Plenary
● Ask the group to tell you what the word 'pair' means.
● Set some simple word problems that require the children to count in twos. For example, count out 16p in 2p coins. Ask: *How many 2p coins did you need?* Take one 2p away and ask: *How much money do you have now?*

Potential difficulties	Further support
Children are not able to count in twos.	Match pairs of gloves. Count in twos to see how many gloves there are altogether.
Children do not understand that a 2p coin has the same value as two 1p coins.	Tap each 2p twice with your finger or exchange each 2p for two 1p coins.

Moving On
● Count on in twos from 1 to familiarise children with the pattern of odd numbers.

Pop to the shop

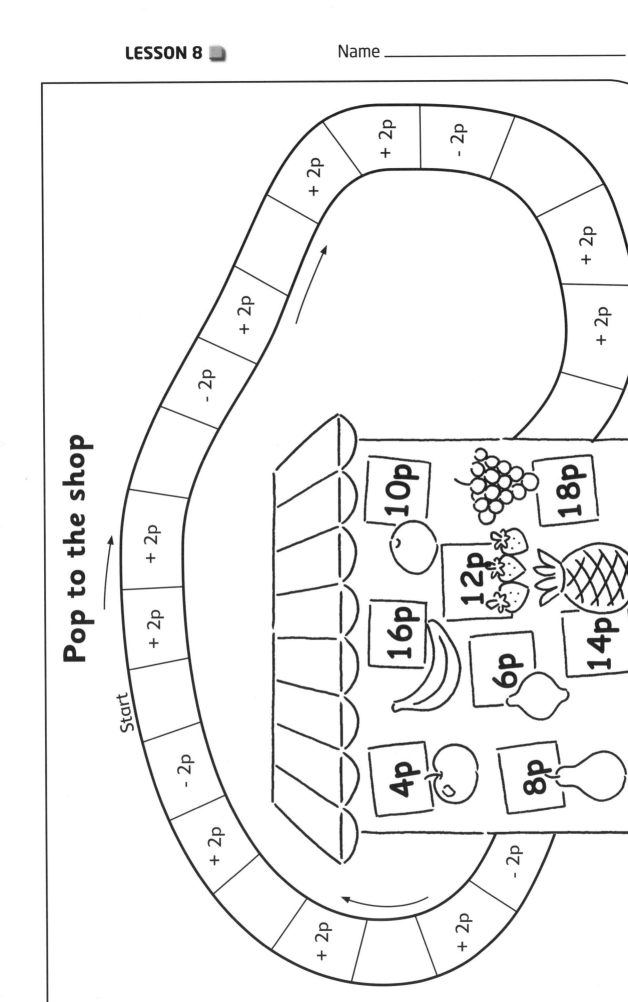

Start

+ 2p
+ 2p
+ 2p
- 2p
+ 2p
+ 2p
+ 2p
+ 2p
- 2p
+ 2p
- 2p
- 2p
+ 2p
+ 2p
+ 2p

10p
18p
12p
16p
6p
14p
4p
8p

LESSON 9

At the bank

Learning objective
(Y1) Begin to know what each digit in a two-digit number represents.
(Y1) Partition a 'teens' number.

Mental starter
See the starter 29 on page 20.

You will need
A set of 'purse and piggy bank' cards from photocopiable page 45; trays of 10p and 1p coins; purses; your role-play area with tables and chairs arranged like the counter in a bank; 1-20 number track.

Moving On
● Extend to amounts above 20p when the children are confident in partitioning teens numbers.

Whole class work
● Show the children the role-play area. Sit behind the counter and pretend that you are a cashier in a bank. Have a simple discussion about why people go to the bank (for example, to withdraw or pay in money).
● Choose one of the children to be a customer at the bank. Give them a purse and one of the purse cards from photocopiable page 45. Explain that you would like them to go to the bank to withdraw the amount of money shown on the card. Demonstrate how to count out the requested amount using 10p and 1p coins.
● Choose a different 'customer' to go to the bank. Give them a piggy bank card. Tell them to count out the amount of money shown on the piggy bank card and take it to the bank to put it in their savings. Model how the banker would check the amount of money and then write out a simple receipt.

Group work
● Plan for the less able children to work in pairs. Allocate the roles of customer and banker. Work alongside the banker, asking questions and making teaching points as necessary. Offer support to children who find it difficult to partition amounts into tens and ones.
● Reinforce how to count on in ones from 10. Demonstrate this practically using a 1-20 number track. Place one 10p coin on the number 10, then place 1p coins over each number until the target number is reached.
● Half way through the activity ask the children in each pair to swap roles.

Plenary
● Put 13p in a purse. Tell the group of less able learners how much money is in the purse. Ask them to show you with their fingers how many 10p coins are in the purse and then how many 1p coins. Repeat for different amounts to see if they have understood how to do this.
● Tell the group that you have put one 10p and four 1p coins in the purse. Ask the children to tell you the total. Repeat for other amounts.

Potential difficulties	Further support
Unable to count on in ones from 10.	Practise counting on in ones from 10 on a number line, 100-square or counting stick.
Children lack understanding of what each digit in a two-digit number represents.	Collect 13 pennies. Exchange ten 1p coins for a 10p coin. Repeat for other amounts.

At the bank

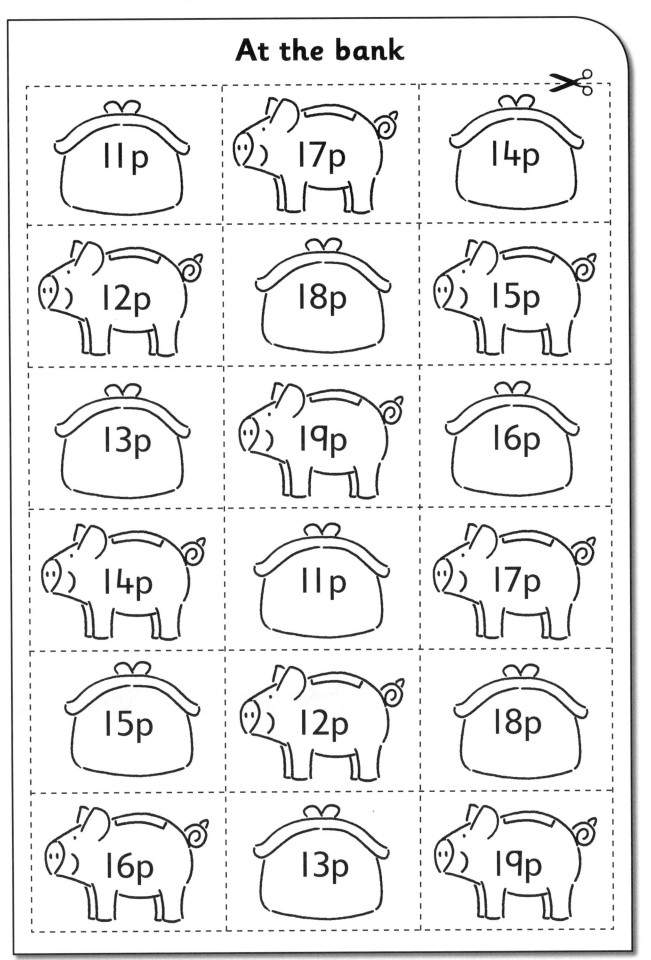

11p

17p

14p

12p

18p

15p

13p

19p

16p

14p

11p

17p

15p

12p

18p

16p

13p

19p

Star collector

Learning objectives
(Y1) Begin to know what each digit in a two-digit number represents.
(Y1) Partition a 'teens' number into a multiple of ten and ones (TU).

Mental starter
See the starter 23 on page 17.

You will need
Photocopiable page 47; arrow cards; counters and several 1-6 dice.

Whole class work

● Tell the children that they are going to practise partitioning two-digit numbers into tens and ones. Explain what a two-digit number is and ask the class to suggest examples of two-digit numbers.

● Draw a rocket on the board. Write the number 16 inside the rocket. Ask the following questions: *Is 16 a two digit number? How do you know? What does the digit 1 stand for? And the 6?*

● Repeat the activity choosing a different child to write a two-digit number in the rocket each time.

Paired work

● Make the number 16 using the arrow cards. Pull the cards apart to illustrate how the number 16 can be partitioned into one ten and six ones. Help the children, in pairs, to represent this visually. One child should hold all their fingers up to represent the 10; their partner should hold 6 fingers up to represent the six ones. Count on together from 10 to 16 to reinforce that one ten and six ones make a total of 16.

● Repeat for other numbers from 10 to 20. Ask the children, in their pairs, to make each number with the arrow cards and then show them how to partition it into a ten and ones on their fingers.

● Give each child a copy of the 'Star collector' game board, 20 counters and a dice. Explain the rules:

1. Each child in a pair takes a turn to roll the dice and move their counter around their own board.

2. Each child then uses arrow cards to make the number they land on and then finds two stars which match the numbers on the arrow cards.

3. They cover the stars with two of their coloured counters.

4. The winner is the first player to use all of their counters.

Plenary

● Write the numbers 10 to 20 on the board. Ask assessment questions such as: *Which number has one ten and seven ones? What does the 5 in 15 stand for?* Let the children use the arrow cards to help them answer the questions.

Potential difficulties	Further support
Children lack understanding of what each digit in a teen number represents.	Focus on the teen numbers in oral and mental starters. Represent the partitioning of teen numbers visually on an abacus.
Children read the digits in a two-digit number as separate single numbers. For example, they partition 16 into 1 and 6 rather than 10 and 6.	Exchange up to 20p practically using 10p and 1p.

Moving On
● Partition larger two-digit numbers.
● Solve missing number problems. For example, *Show me the number we add to 10 to make 16.*

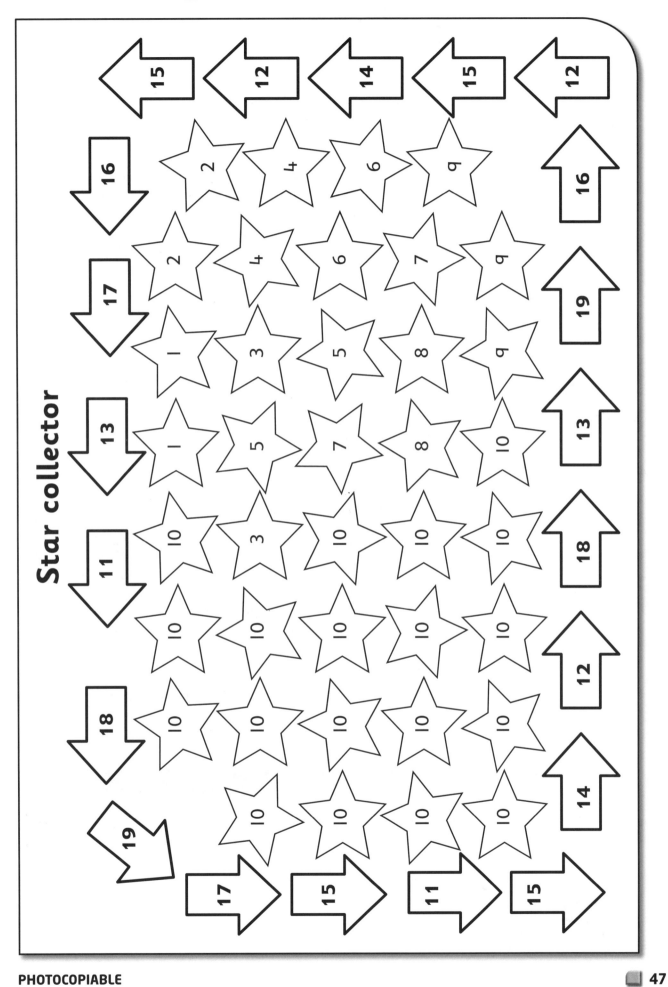

Star collector

Zero the hero

Learning objective
(Y1) Begin to know what each digit in a two-digit number represents.

Mental starter
See the starter, 46 on page 26.

You will need
Several copies of photocopiable page 49 for paired work; A3-sized number cards (0-9); Multilink cubes; 1-9 spinners (see photocopiable page 49); different coloured counters; a set of place-value cards per pair (number ten units only); a 100-square.

Whole class work

● Pick two children to hold the number cards 1 and 0. Instruct them to join the cards together so that the digits read as 10. Explain that zero is a 'hero' because it is a place-holder; the number 10 is made up of one ten and no ones (the zero is 'saving the ones place').
● Hold up a stick of 10 cubes and ask: *Who do you think should hold the 10 cubes? The 1 or the zero? Why? Do we need to give the zero some cubes to hold?*
● Explain that without zero it would not be possible to make the number 10. Ask the children to identify other numbers on the 100-square which could not be made without the help of 'Zero the hero'!

Group work

● Hold up 6 cubes in front of the group. Count on from 10 the number of cubes you are holding up. Say: *one ten and six ones makes 16.*
● Remind the children that zero was important in the number 10 because there were no ones. Now there are six ones.
● Hold up the number cards 1 and 0 so they read 10. Give a child the number 6 card. Tell them to replace your zero card with their number 6 to change the 10 into 16.
● Model the inverse operation. If the six ones are taken away, Zero the hero is still there saving the 'ones' place'.
● Make other teen numbers in this way.

Paired work

● Split the children into pairs. Give each pair a game board, two sets of different coloured counters, a 1-9 spinner (see photocopiable page 49) and a set of single digit place-value cards.
● Players take it in turns to roll the dice, place the corresponding place-value card over the zero on the number 10 and then cover the two-digit number they have made on the board with a counter.
● The winner is the child with the most counters on the board at the end of the game.

Plenary

● Use place-value cards to demonstrate adding a single digit to 10 (or other multiples of 10). Chant the number sentences together, for example: *10 + 4 = 14; 10 + 3 = 13.* Invite individual children to chant them out alone.

Potential difficulties	Further support
Children do not understand what each digit in a two-digit number represents.	Use place-value cards to make two-digit numbers. Say how many tens/ones are in each number.

Moving On
● Add single digit numbers to other multiples of 10.

Ze...

12	14				
19	15	16			8
13	15	16	19	12	18
15	14	13	16	17	11
17	16	17	12	18	13
18	19	11	15	19	14

(handwritten note) Enlarge the spinner for the c4 to use. Laminate copies of this sheet.

Make a difference - TEACH

Lancashire County Council

Teacher Recruitment and Retention Team
Tel: 01772 531885 www.teachinglin.lancashire.gov.uk

◼ Copy onto card. Cut out spinner and pierce centre with a pencil.

Snake race

Learning objectives
(Y1) Understand and use the vocabulary of comparing and ordering numbers.
(Y1) Compare two familiar numbers, say which is more or less.

Mental starter
See the starter 31 on page 21.

You will need
The game board on photocopiable page 51 and a set of 0-20 number cards per pair for the less able children; red and blue crayons and counters; dice labelled 'more'/ 'less'; large 0-20 number track.

Whole class work

● Count along the number track from 0 to 20 and back again. Ask the class to identify the smallest and the largest numbers they said. Were the numbers getting more or less each time?
● Choose two children. Give them each a number card and ask them to locate the position of their number on the 0-20 number track. Ask the children to say which of the two numbers they think is more/bigger or less/smaller. How did they know this?
● Encourage and support the children in using correct mathematical vocabulary when answering questions and offering explanations.

Paired work

● Divide the less able group into pairs to play the 'Snake race' game on photocopiable page 51.
How to play
1. The children in each pair decide whether to be red or blue.
2. Both players take a number card and place their counter on the number they have picked.
3. Next they roll the more/less dice. If it lands on 'more' the person whose counter is on the larger number scores a point and if it lands on 'less' the person with their counter on the smaller number scores a point. Demonstrate how the children can use the more/less arrow underneath the number track to help them.
4. Each player colours a segment of the snake in their colour (red or blue) every time they score a point.
5. The game is over when the snake is completely coloured. The player with the most segments of their colour is the winner.

Plenary

● Split the less able group into two teams.
● Deal each team a card from the 0-20 number card pile and ask them to roll the more/less dice. Can the children work out which team scores a point without referring to the number line?
● The first team to score 5 points is the winner. At the end of the activity, select specific children to explain how they know a number is 'more' or 'less' out of two given numbers.

Potential difficulties	Further support
Children have difficulty with the vocabulary 'more', 'less' and so on.	Use concrete apparatus. Compare sets of objects in practical contexts, (*Who has more sweets/pennies, and so on?*). Simplify the lesson by asking children to identify the number that is 'more' every time. Adapt the game accordingly.

Moving On
● Say which number is more or less without the aid of a number line.
● Compare and order numbers to 100.

Snake race

A game for two players.
You will need:
- a set of number cards 0-20
- one red counter and one blue counter
- a red crayon and a blue crayon
- a dice labelled more, more, more, less, less, less

1	2	3	4	5	6	7	8	9	10	11	12	13	14	15	16	17	18	19	20

less ← → more

Piggy in the middle

Learning objectives
(Y1) Understand and use the vocabulary of comparing and ordering numbers.
(Y1) Compare two familiar numbers and give a number which lies between them.

Mental starter
See the starter, 39 on page 23.

You will need
0-20 number cards; laminated copy of photocopiable page 53 per group; three pig headbands (attach two ear shapes to a strip of pink card); 5-minute sand timer or stopwatch.

Whole class work

● Play 'Piggy in the Middle' with the class - pick three children to stand up and put on the pig headbands. Deal each 'little pig' a number card and ask them to hold it up.

● Ask the class to compare the three numbers. Can they identify the smallest and the largest numbers? Invite a child to tell the little pigs where to stand so that the three numbers are sequenced in order from smallest to largest. Explain that the second pig in line is the 'piggy in the middle' because their number lies *between* the other two numbers.

● Check this by counting on in ones from the smallest to the largest number or by looking at the numbers on a number line.

● Let the 'piggy in the middle' stay and choose different children to wear the other headbands. Deal three new number cards and repeat the game until all the children have had a turn at being a pig.

Group work

● Organise the less able children to work in small groups. Provide each group with a laminated copy of 'Piggy in the middle', a set of 0-20 number cards and a whiteboard pen.

● Invite a child in each group to turn over two number cards. Ask them to place the smallest number on the first pig and the largest number on the third pig.

● Another member of the group should then write a number which they think lies between these two numbers on the 'piggy in the middle'.

● Within their groups, ask the children to count together in ones from the smallest to the largest number to check the numbers are sequenced correctly. If the number order is correct, the group may award themselves a point.

● Supervise the children to check that they understand which numbers should be placed in the middle. Provide 100-squares for children who are struggling.

Plenary

● Repeat the whole class game with the less able learners group but this time vary the rules by asking the children to identify the largest number first (working from largest to smallest).

Potential difficulties	Further support
Children are unable to order numbers correctly.	Simplify the group activity. Give each group two pigs cut from the photocopiable sheet and ask them to order two numbers from smallest to largest.
Children cannot think of a number that lies inbetween.	Provide number lines for children to refer to.

Moving On
● Copy and cut out four little pigs. Stick the pigs in a line on the board. Develop the whole class activity by asking children to suggest two numbers that lie between two given numbers.

Piggy in the middle

Traffic jam

Learning objectives
(Y1) Order numbers from 0 to at least 20.
(Y1) Count reliably at least 20 objects.

Mental starter
See the starter, 18 on page 15.

You will need
Photocopiable page 55 - copy and cut out a set of 20 vehicle cards per group plus one set of 20 enlarged vehicle cards for teacher demonstration; a set of 1-20 number cards per group.

Whole class work
● Practise ordering and counting numbers up to 20. Stick the 20 vehicle cards in a line on the board. Ask a child to point to the vehicle which is *first* in the traffic jam. Count the total number of vehicles in the jam.
● Next, ask individual children to number the vehicles in the traffic jam from 1 to 20 by picking a number card and placing it under the correct vehicle. Demonstrate how to do this by counting in ones from the first vehicle.
● Count together to check the numbers have been ordered correctly.

Group work
● Repeat the whole class activity with the less able group. Next position a few numbers correctly and ask individual children to place the remaining numbers under the vehicles. Ask them to explain how they did this. For example, *I know this car is number 5 because 5 is the number that comes after 4.*
● Now order 20 vehicle cards in front of the group of children and place the corresponding number cards underneath them. Ask the children to close their eyes. Swap two of the cars and their numbers over. Challenge the children to spot which two cars have changed position. The first person to answer correctly should return the two numbers and vehicles to the correct position.

Paired work
● Give each pair of children a set of vehicle cards and a set of 1-20 number cards. Tell them to arrange the vehicle cards in a line and then number the vehicles in order from 1 to 20.
● In their pairs, ask one child to close their eyes while their partner swaps two numbers over. Each time a child correctly identifies which two numbers have been switched they score a point. The child with the most points when the activity is over wins the game.

Plenary
● Ask the children in the group to close their eyes. Remove one of the vehicles from the traffic jam. Ask the children to shout out which car has gone.
● Ask them to explain how they knew the answer.

Potential difficulties	Further support
Children have difficulty reading and ordering numbers 11 to 19.	Reduce the number of vehicles in the traffic jam to 10.
Children cannot recite the numbers from 0 to 20 in order.	Practise counting backwards in oral and mental starters using a counting stick or number line.

Moving On
● Number the vehicles from 20 to one to provide an opportunity to practise counting backwards in ones.
● Number 5 vehicles in order, using a set of numbers in the range 0 to 20, such as: 3, 5, 6, 9, 14.

Traffic jam

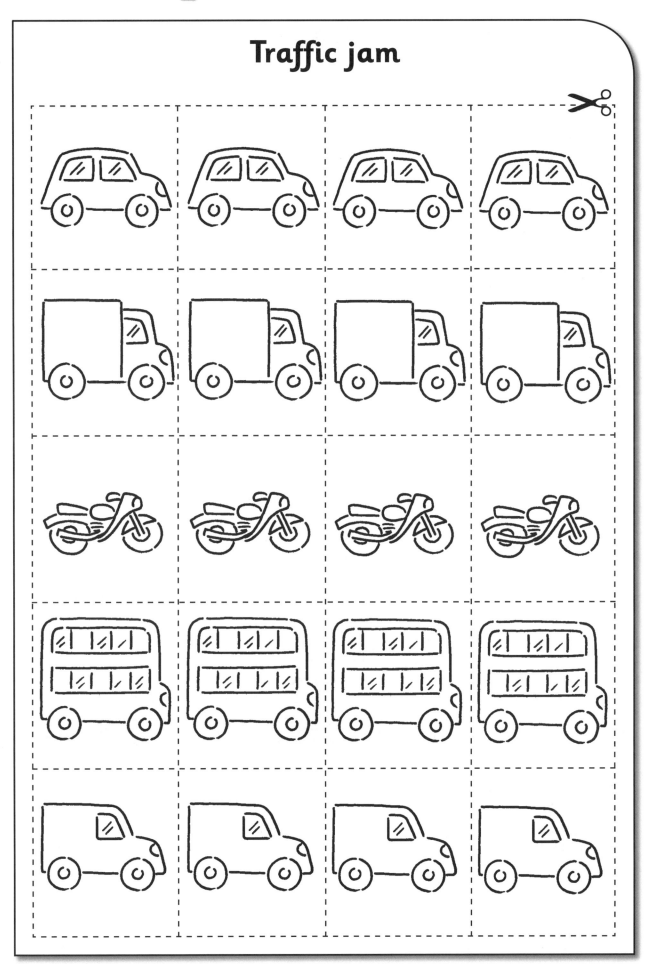

Youngest to oldest

Learning objective
(Y1) Order numbers to at least 20.

Mental starter
See the starter 26 on page 19.

You will need
Photocopiable page 57, one per child (write a different number on each of the cakes to indicate the ages of the toys); six soft toys each wearing a badge to show their age (2, 7, 3, 9, 1, 4); a number line (1–10).

Whole class work

- Hold up one of the toys and ask the children to tell you its age by reading its badge.
- Lead the children counting from zero until they reach the age of the toy. Point to the numbers on a number line as the children count. Repeat with each of the toys.
- Ask the children to say which toy is the oldest and which is the youngest and explain how they know.

Group work

- Give each child a toy to hold. Tell the children that you would like them to arrange the toys in age order from youngest to oldest.
- Ask the child who is holding the youngest toy to bring it to the front. If necessary, explain that the youngest toy has the smallest number on its badge. Continue until all the toys are arranged in a line.
- Invite the children to count in ones from zero until they reach the number on the badge of the oldest toy. Tell them that whenever you hear a number which is on one of the toys' badges you are going to turn that toy around. Explain that if you turn the toys around in the order that they are lined up, then that means that the children have completed the task correctly.
- Invite the children to come and circle the ages of each of the toys on a number line. This will provide a more visual method of demonstrating whether the toys are ordered correctly.

Independent work

- Give all the children a copy of photocopiable page 57. Tell the children that you would like them to cut out the pictures of the toys and arrange them in age order starting with the youngest toy.
- Encourage them to check their work using the counting and number line strategies modelled during the group work.

Plenary

- Sequence the toys in order, youngest to oldest. Tell the group to close their eyes. Swap two of the toy's badges over. Challenge the children to identify which two numbers have been changed.

Potential difficulties	Further support
Children find it difficult to order six numbers.	Ask the children to sequence just three toys or pictures at a time.
The children are unable to order non-consecutive numbers.	Order a set of consecutive numbers.

Moving On
- Order numbers within the range 0 to 100.
- Compare the ages of two toys and say which is the oldest/youngest. Place a toy between them. Invite the children to guess the age of the toy by suggesting a number which lies between the two known numbers.

Youngest to oldest

Cut out the pictures.

■ Stick the toys in the correct order starting with the youngest toy.

Pizza toppings

Learning objectives
(YR) Begin to relate addition to combining two groups of objects.
(Y1) Begin to use the +, -, and = signs to record mental calculations in a number sentence.

Mental starter
See the starter 'Two hand draw' on page 16.

You will need
A set of pizza topping cards (from photocopiable page 59), a dice and a paper plate for each child; a large card pizza base and an enlarged set of pizza topping cards.

Whole class work
● Pick two children to play 'Two hand draw' (see the starter activity, page 16).
● Write a number sentence on the board to represent the number of fingers the children are holding up, for example: 5 + 2 = 7.
● Repeat the activity with other pairs of children. Make sure that the class understand the meaning of the plus and equals symbols.

Group work
● Ask the children to sit in a circle around the giant pizza base. Tell the children that you would like them to help you create a pizza with two different toppings.
● Ask a child to choose a topping to put on the pizza such as pepper. Ask them to roll the dice and then count that many pieces of pepper onto the pizza.
● Pick a different child to select and add a second topping to the pizza in the same way.
● Recall how many pieces of each topping were added to the pizza. Count how many pieces of topping are on the pizza altogether, using a variety of related vocabulary. For example, there are 5 pieces of pepper *and/plus* 4 pieces of ham; that makes 9 toppings *altogether*.
● Demonstrate how to write this as a number sentence: 5 + 4 = 9.
● Create other pizzas in this way. Encourage the children to describe each pizza using appropriate vocabulary.

Independent work
● Give each child a set of their own pizza topping cards, a dice and a paper plate.
● Instruct them to create different pizzas and write a number sentence to match each pizza. Provide support as required, especially with the writing of number sentences.

Plenary
● Write a number sentence on the board, such as: 4 + 2 = 6. Ask the children from the less able group to use their individual pizzas to create a pizza to match the number sentence.
● Check to see if everyone has done this correctly. Repeat this several times.

Potential difficulties	Further support
Children do not relate the combining of two different sets to how many objects there are altogether.	Limit the children to one topping per pizza. Roll the dice twice and add two lots of the chosen topping. Count how many pieces of topping there are altogether.
Counting is inaccurate when the cards are arranged randomly on the pizza.	Model how to remove the cards from the pizza one by one as they are counted.

Moving On
● Make pizzas with three different toppings, count all the pieces to find the total.

Pizza toppings

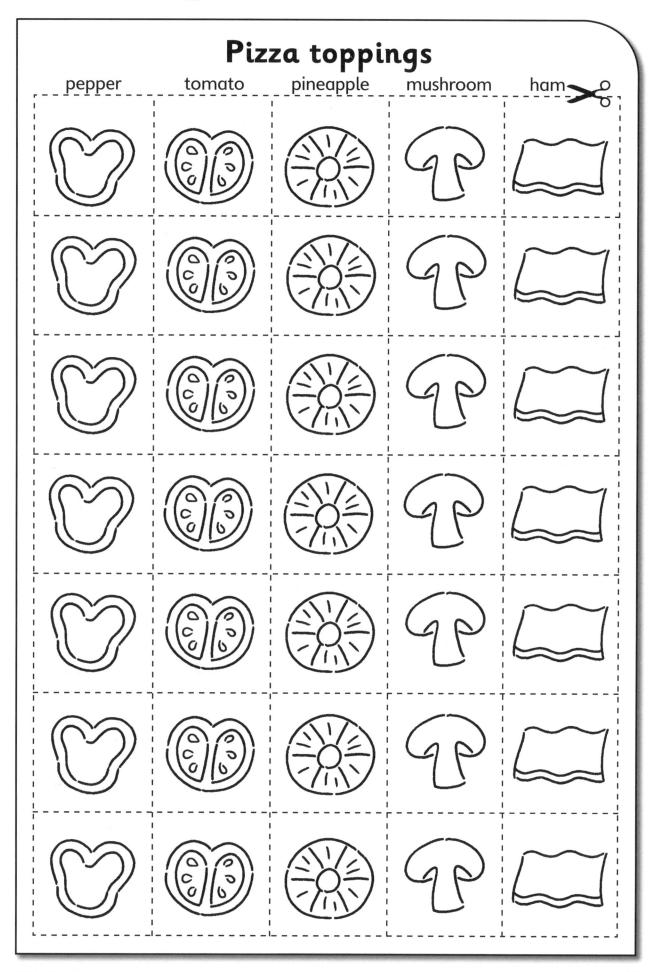

Birthday candles

Learning objective
(Y1) Know by heart all pairs of numbers with a total of 10.
(Y1) Solve simple mathematical problems and puzzles.

Mental starter
See the starter 25 on page 18.

You will need
A laminated copy of photocopiable page 61 per child in the less able group; a teddy bear; pegs; birthday badges; two simple cardboard cake shapes attached to a shoe box (to help them stand upright).

Whole class work

● Tell the children that today is Teddy's birthday. Challenge them to guess how old he is (8). Give Teddy a number 8 badge to wear. Ask the children to say whether Teddy is older or younger than they are.

● Tell the children that Teddy has invited so many toys to his birthday party that he has had to make two cakes. Reveal the two cardboard cakes. Explain that Teddy would like the children to help him work out how he could arrange his birthday candles on the two cakes.

● With the class, count out 8 pegs to represent the 8 candles. Clip the candles onto the two cakes in any arrangement. Discuss the arrangement of the candles with the children.

Group work

● Repeat this activity in detail with the group of less able learners. Ask each child to clip the candles on the cake in a different arrangement. Discuss the different arrangements of 8 that are possible. Such discussion will provide opportunities to reinforce one to one correspondence when counting and to model the appropriate use of key mathematical vocabulary.

Independent work

● Give each child a laminated copy of photocopiable page 61. Tell them to write Teddy's age in the box at the top of the page. Ask them to investigate different ways of separating 8 candles onto the two cakes by drawing candles with a dry-wipe pen. Supervise and assist the children where necessary.

Plenary

● Working with the group, peg some of the 8 candles onto the first cake. Challenge the children to work out how many candles need to be put on the second cake to make a total of 8 candles.

● Encourage the children to model different arrangements by using their fingers to help them.

Potential difficulties	Further support
The children are insecure with facts to 10 as they have not progressed from facts to 5.	Simplify the activity by using fewer candles.
Not able to record correctly on the laminated sheet.	Give pairs of children two cardboard cakes and 8 pegs. Ask them to investigate different ways of splitting the candles into two groups practically. This will help avoid recording errors, such as drawing too many candles.

Moving On
● Repeat the activity for other numbers to 10 to reinforce number bonds.
● Focus on missing number problems: *Teddy is 10 years old. If he puts 4 candles on one cake, how many candles will he need to put on the other cake to make 10?*

Birthday candles

HAPPY BIRTHDAY

HAPPY BIRTHDAY

How many apples?

Learning objective
(Y1) Understand the operation of addition.

Mental starter
See the starter 12 on page 13.

You will need
Laminated copies of photocopiable page 63 (one per child in the less able group plus an enlarged A3 copy for demonstration); a small basket; 20 apples; dry-wipe pens; 1-6 dice.

Whole class work

● Place 5 apples into the basket. Ask a child to record how many apples are inside the basket by writing the corresponding numeral in the empty box on the enlarged photocopiable.
● Add 1 more apple to the basket. Ask: *Who can change the number on the basket to show how many apples there are now?*
● Add 2 more apples to the basket and ask them what the total is. Model how to count on from the number of apples already in the basket using the 1-20 apple number line on the photocopiable.
● Continue adding apples to the basket, a few at a time until all 20 apples are in the basket.

Group work

● Organise the less able learners into groups of two or three to play 'How many apples?'.

How to play

1. Give each child their own laminated copy of the 'How many apples?' photocopiable.
2. Each player rolls the dice to determine the number of apples in their basket at the start of the game.
3. Players take it in turns to roll the dice, add that number of apples to their basket and change the number on their basket accordingly.
4. The first player to collect 20 apples wins the game.
● Remind the children how to calculate the total number of apples by counting on in steps of one from the number of apples already in the basket. Show the children how they can use the 1-20 apple number line on the photocopiable to help them.

Plenary

● Set some simple problems for the less able group. For example, say: *I have 5 apples in my basket. If I put 3 more apples in the basket, how many apples will I have altogether?*
● Encourage different children to demonstrate and explain how they were able to find the total. Support children who have difficulty explaining.

Moving On
● Challenge children to be the first to collect 30 or more apples.
● Teach the children to count on to calculate how many more are needed to make a total, asking questions such as: *There are 5 apples in the basket how many more do I need to make a total of 8 apples altogether?*

Potential difficulties	Further support
Children make errors when counting on by making jumps on a number line.	Provide each child with a counter to help them keep track of each step they make on the number line.

Name ____________________

How many apples?

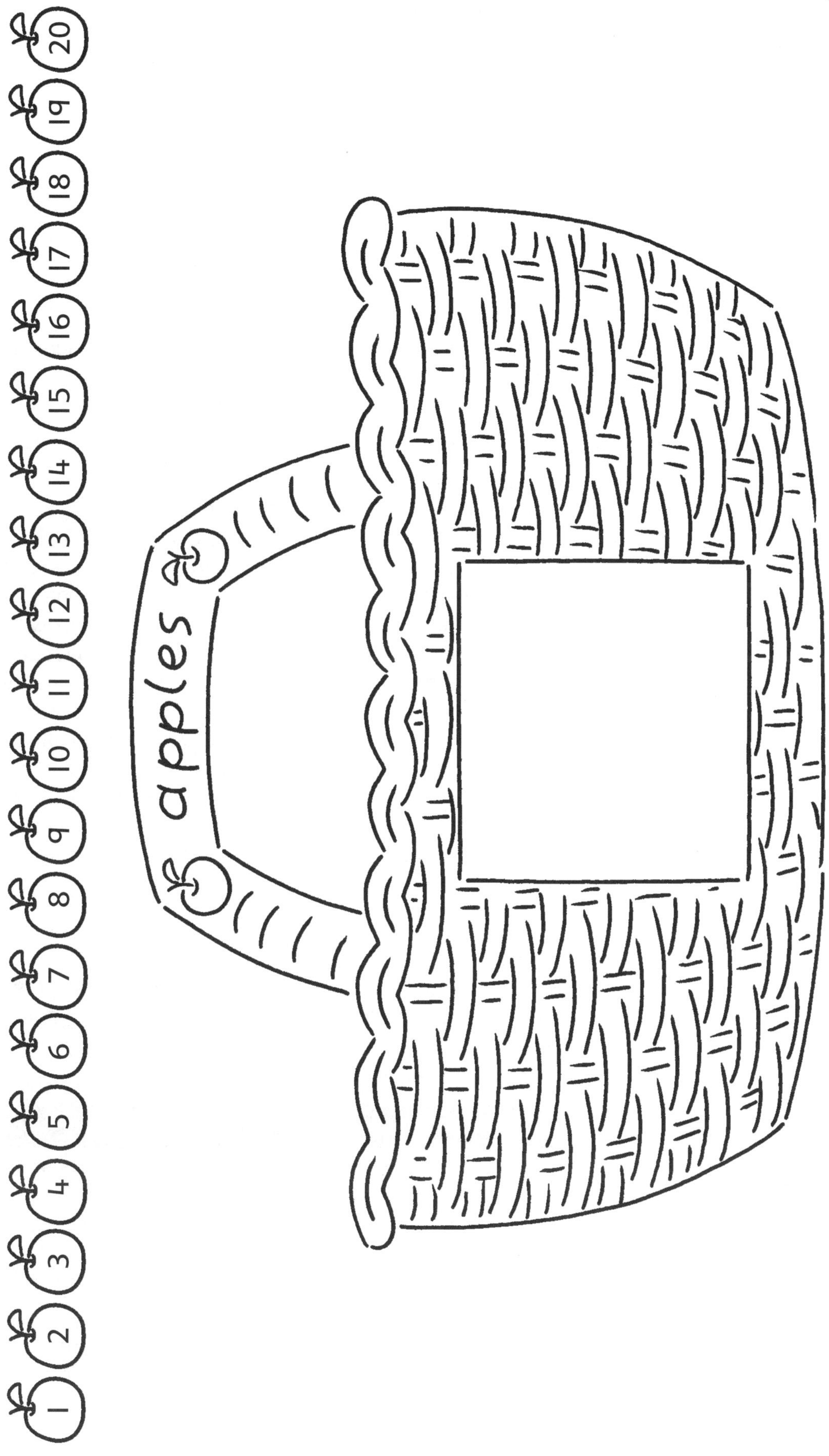

Largest first

Learning objectives
(Y2) Use knowledge that addition can be done in any order to do mental calculations more efficiently.

Mental starter
See the starter 43 on page 25.

You will need
Photocopiable page 65 for each pair of children; several 1-6 dice; blank dice labelled 10-15; 0-20 number cards.

Whole class work
- Roll two 1-6 dice. Model how to add the numbers together by holding one of the numbers in your head and then counting on.
- Divide the class into two groups. Roll both dice again. Challenge the children to add the two numbers as quickly as they can by counting on. Ask each group to add the numbers in a different order (for example, either 5 count on 3 or 3 count on 5).
- Explain that because both groups arrive at the same answer, addition can be done in any order. Repeat the activity.
- Now roll a 1-6 dice and a 10-15 dice. Ask the children to add the numbers together, each group adding the numbers in a different order. For example, 5 + 10 and 10 + 5. Discuss why the group who started with the largest number were able to work out the answer more quickly.

Paired work
Organise the less-able group into pairs. Each pair will need a score card from photocopiable page 65, a 1-6 dice and a 10-15 dice.
- Tell the children to take it in turns to roll the dice, add the two numbers together and then write the total in the appropriate box on the score card. Model how to use the largest/smallest boxes at the top of the photocopiable sheet to order the dice 'largest' first before adding the numbers together. Explain that each time both dice are thrown, the children should place the dice showing the largest number, in the box labelled 'largest' on the photocopiable sheet and the other dice in the 'smallest' box.
- Suggest that the children compare their scores after each round. The player with the highest total for each round can colour in a smiley face.
- Provide number lines to support children who cannot add the numbers by counting on in their heads. Alternatively let the children simply count the spots on each dice.

Plenary
Hold up two number cards and ask the children to add the numbers together as quickly as they can. Pick different children to demonstrate how they were able to do this. Ask them to remind you why is it quicker to start from the largest number.

Potential difficulties	Further support
Children are not able to say which of two numbers is the largest.	Provide 0-20 number lines for children to refer to.
Children are unable to find a total by counting on because they are unsure of the next number in the number sequence.	Have number tracks available. Demonstrate how to add two numbers by counting on in ones from the largest number.

Moving On
- Set the children some simple addition problems (see 'At the Café' page 102). Observe how the children calculate the answers. Do they put the larger number first without prompting?

Largest first

	Largest	Smallest
	☐	☐
	Player 1	Player 2

	name	name
Round 1	☐ ☺	☐ ☺
Round 2	☐ ☺	☐ ☺
Round 3	☐ ☺	☐ ☺
Round 4	☐ ☺	☐ ☺
Round 5	☐ ☺	☐ ☺
Round 6	☐ ☺	☐ ☺
Round 7	☐ ☺	☐ ☺

50 MATHS LESSONS · AGES 5-7

Lucky dip

Learning objectives
(Y1) Begin to recognise that more than two numbers can be added together.
(Y1) Begin to use the +, -, and = signs to record mental calculations in a number sentence.

Mental starter
See the starter 17 on page 15.

You will need
Four sets of 'Lucky dip picture cards' (from photocopiable page 67); four lucky dip/party bags; a lucky dip bag containing 5 pencils, 3 sweets and 4 toy cars; dice; paper and pencils.

Whole class work
● Hold up the lucky dip bag and ask the children to guess what might be inside it. Invite individuals to take it in turns to pick an object out of the bag. Tell them to place the objects in categories on a table near you. Continue until the bag is empty. Ask: *How many sweets/pencils/cars were in the bag? How many things were in the bag altogether? How did you work it out?*
● Show the children how to write the calculation as a number sentence on the board (5 + 3 + 4 = 12). Discuss the meaning of each symbol and model appropriate vocabulary: *5 pencils plus 3 sweets plus 4 cars equals 12 objects altogether.*

Group work
● Stick one set of 'Lucky dip picture cards' on the board. Choose a child to roll the dice and then count that many pencil picture cards into a bag. Pick further children to roll the dice and add the appropriate numbers of sweet and car cards.
● Then select a child to empty out the bag, sort the cards and count how many there are altogether. Write a number sentence on the board to represent the calculation. Make sure the children understand the notation.
● Repeat this activity several times.

Paired work
● Give each pair of children one set of lucky dip picture cards and one lucky dip bag. Ask them to repeat the group activity. This time, provide paper and pencils to encourage the children to record their mental calculations as number sentences.
● Work alongside individual children. Ask them to read out the number sentences they have made and explain what they mean using appropriate vocabulary.

Plenary
● Copy a number sentence made by one of the less able pairs onto the board and challenge the rest of the group to calculate the total.
● Ask them to explain the strategy they used to work the answer out, for example, using their picture cards, counting on their fingers or mentally by counting on.
● Repeat for different number sentences.

Potential difficulties	Further support
Unable to set out the number sentence correctly.	Provide children with a template of a number sentence copied onto a laminated sheet for them to re-use.

Moving On
● Teach the strategy of adding three numbers mentally by counting on.
● Challenge the children to see how many ways they can make a total of 12 using three numbers.

Lucky dip

50 MATHS LESSONS · AGES 5-7

Hook a duck

Learning objective
(Y1) Begin to recognise that more than two numbers can be added together.

Mental starter
See the starter 'Two hand draw' on page 16.

You will need
'Hook a Duck' photocopiable, one per child; paperclips; a 'fishing rod' made by tying a small magnet to a piece of string.

Whole class work

● Develop the starter activity by organising the children into groups of three to play 'Three hand draw'. Instruct the children on an agreed signal to draw one hand out from behind their back with some fingers held up. Tell each group to count how many fingers they are holding up altogether.

● Encourage the children to put one of the numbers in their head and then count on in ones until they have reached the total number of fingers held up.

Group work

● Ask the children in the less able group to sit in a circle. Give each child a copy of the prize list from the 'Hook a duck' photocopiable page 69.

● Tell the children that you are going to play a game called 'Hook a duck'. Ask them to look at the prizes they can win on their prize boards.

● Cut up a set of duck cards, attach a paperclip to each one, and spread them face down on the floor in the middle of the circle. Choose a child to hook three ducks with the magnetic fishing rod. Stick the ducks on the board.

● Work with the children to add the three duck numbers together. Look on the prize list to see if the child has scored enough points to win one of the prizes.

● Let other children play the game. Tell the children to colour in each prize they win.

● Support children who find it hard to mentally add together three small numbers. Show them how to hold one of the numbers in their head and then count on their fingers to add the other two numbers.

Plenary

● Show the less able children the three ducks numbered 2, 2 and 3. Ask: *Can you see a pair of numbers that you can add in your head?* For example, *I know double 2 makes 4.*

● Discuss how, by using their knowledge of known number facts, children may be able to add three numbers more easily.

Moving On
● Adapt the game by writing larger numbers on the ducks and adjusting the number of points required to win each prize.
● Teach mental strategies to help children add three numbers more efficiently. For example, encourage the children to identify doubles or pairs of numbers which make 10 within a set of three numbers.

Potential difficulties	Further support
Children are unable to add three small numbers together mentally by counting on.	Draw the appropriate number of dots on each duck. Tell children to count the dots to check their answers. Demonstrate how to add three small numbers by making jumps on a 0-10 number line.

Name _____

Hook a duck

■ Have you won a prize?

Ten little lollipops

Learning objectives
(Y1) Understand the operation of subtraction as 'take away'.
(Y1) Solve simple problems set in 'real life'.

Mental starter
See the starter, 21 on page 17.

You will need
Photocopiable page 71, copied onto thin card (one per pair of children and an enlarged A3 copy for demonstration); 0-10 number cards; a bag containing 10 lollipops; a washing line.

Whole class work

● Stick the unordered set of 0-10 number cards on the board. Hold up the bag of lollipops. Let the children take turns to hold the bag and guess how many lollipops are inside.
● Next, count the lollipops altogether. Emphasize one-to-one correspondence by holding up each lollipop in turn as the children count. Ask a child to locate number 10 on the board and peg it onto a washing line.
● Teach the children the rhyme 'Ten little lollipops'.
Ten little lollipops in the sweetie shop. Take a little lollipop and off you pop!
Nine little lollipops... (and so on, until):
Zero little lollipops in the sweetie shop. They've all been eaten up so off you pop!
● After each verse, pause, choose a child to take one of the lollipops away and then count how many remain. Locate the appropriate number card and peg it on the washing line. Continue the rhyme until there are no lollipops left.
● At the end of the rhyme count back with the children from 10 to 0. Point to the numbers on the washing line in order as the children count backwards.

Group work

● Hold up the A3-sized lollipop strip (from photocopiable page 71) in front of the group. Ask the children to count the total number of lollipops on the strip.
● Tell the children that you are going to let them each have a turn to come to your sweet shop to get some lollipops. Choose who will go first. Say: *I have 10 little lollipops in my sweetie shop, take (say, 4) little lollipops and off you pop!* Ask the child to select the matching number card from the set of 0-10 number cards. Demonstrate how to lower the appropriate number of flaps on the strip of lollipops. Talk about what has been done. For example: *I started with 10 lollipops, Joe took away 4 of them. Let's count how many I have left: 1, 2, 3, 4, 5, 6.*
● Let everyone in the group have at least one turn to come to the shop.

Plenary

● Ask each child in the group to make up a simple subtraction word problem. The rest of the group must solve the problem with their lollipop strip/fingers.

Moving On
● Teach children to record simple subtractions using the - and = signs.
● Use complementary addition to work out the answers to simple problems. For example: *I had 10 lollipops in the shop. At the end of the day I had 5 left. How many did I sell?*

Potential difficulties	Further support
Some children are unable to count back from 10 to 0.	Practise counting backwards using a number line.

Ten little lollipops

Colourful caterpillars

Learning objective
(Y1) Understand the operation of addition, and of subtraction (as 'take away', 'difference'), and use the related vocabulary.

Mental starter
See the starter 44 on page 25.

You will need
Photocopiable page 73; two sets of coloured counters; a 1-9 dice or a spinner; two colours of Multilink cubes per pair of children; a bag containing nine stripy caterpillars ranging in length from 1 to 9 Multilink cubes.

Whole class work
● Pick two caterpillars out of the bag (such as 7 and 5). Tell the children that you are going to show them how to work out the difference between the number of cubes which have been used to make each caterpillar.
● Place the caterpillars side by side. Count how many more cubes have been used to make the longer caterpillar. Explain that the difference between the lengths of the caterpillars is two cubes.

Group work
● Invite individuals in the group to pull two caterpillars from the bag and work out the difference between their lengths. Encourage the children to describe their method and explain how they could make both caterpillars the same length by either adding or subtracting cubes.

Paired work
● Teach the children how to play the 'Colourful caterpillar' game.
● Provide each pair with a game board (photocopiable page 73), a 1-9 dice or spinner, two colours of counters.
● First show the children how to use the cubes to make their own set of nine stripy caterpillars ranging in length from 1 to 9 cubes. Explain the rules of the game:
1. Decide who will start.
2. Roll the dice and locate the caterpillar with the corresponding number of cubes. Do this again. (Note: if a player shakes the same number twice they must miss a go.)
3. Work out the difference in length between the two caterpillars. Use a counter to cover that number on the board.
4. The winner is the player who has the most counters on the board at the end of the game (when the caterpillar is all covered up).

Plenary
● Revise the term 'difference' with the class. Ask them to tell you how they can find the difference between two numbers.
● Ask questions such as: *If my caterpillar had 9 spots and your caterpillar had 5, what would the difference be?* Work out the answers on a number line if necessary.

Potential difficulties	Further support
Children have difficulty recognising and using the vocabulary of subtraction.	Model the use of a variety of words such as: *How many less, take away, difference* and so on.
Children do not relate finding the difference to taking away.	Make two caterpillars the same length by breaking off the 'extra' cubes from the longer one. Explain that these cubes represent the 'difference' between the caterpillars.

Moving On
● Teach the children how to solve missing number problems using concrete apparatus or a number line.

Colourful caterpillars

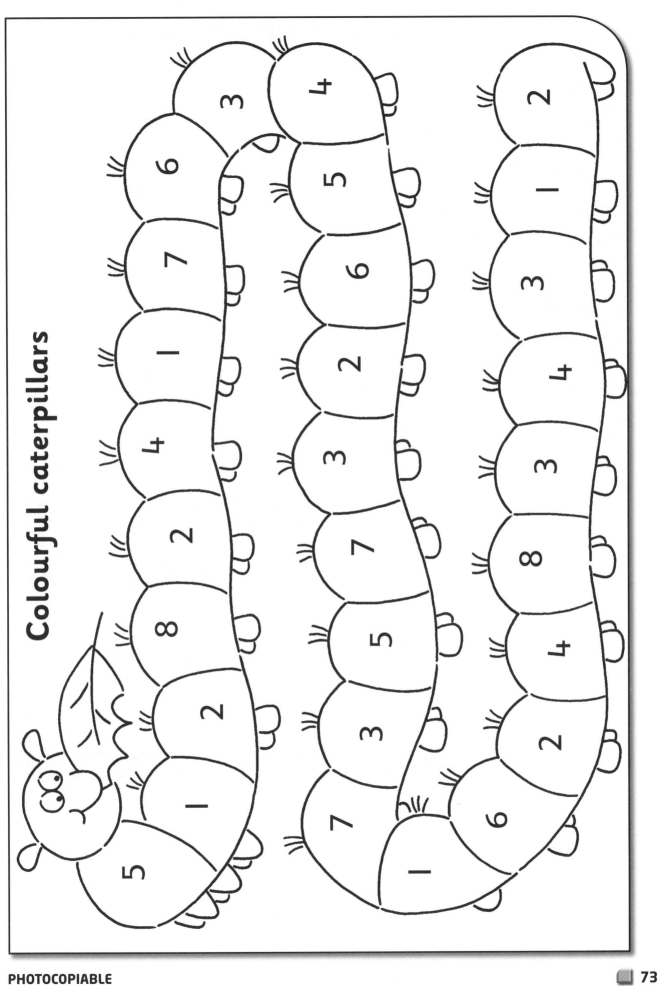

Shopkeeper's change

Learning objective
(Y2) Find a small difference by counting up from the smaller to the larger number.

Mental starter
See the starter 33 on page 21.

You will need
Photocopiable page 75; eight small toys priced from 12p-19p; 20p coins; one pence coins; number fans.

Whole class work

● Lay out 12 pennies in a line. Show the toy priced 15p. Ask: *Do I have enough money to buy this toy?* Add 'extra' pennies to the line until there are 15. Ask the class to count how many more pennies you needed to add to 12p to make 15p.

● Leave the 15 pennies on the table. Hold up the toy priced 18p. Model how to calculate how many more pennies you need to buy the toy by counting on from the smaller to the larger number. Tap the toy as you say the start number and then hold up one finger at a time to represent each of the 'extra' ones counted.

● Repeat the activity several times. Select a different child to explain how they calculated the answer each time.

Group work

● Put all of the toys on the table. Ask one child to choose a toy to buy and pay for it with a 20p. Explain that because the toy costs less than 20p you must give the child some change. Demonstrate how to calculate the change by counting on as before.

● Let each child in the group have a turn to buy a toy and to be the shopkeeper.

Paired work

● Give each pair of children a copy of photocopiable page 75, some 20p and some 1p coins. Tell the children to take it in turns to point to something they would like to buy on the sheet and pay for it with a 20p coin. Their partner should work out how much change they need by counting up from the price to 20p.

● Observe how the children work the answers out. Talk to the children about their work and use a variety of mathematical vocabulary such as: *difference, how many more, how many extra*.

Plenary

● Write the numbers 25 and 29 on the board. Ask the group to calculate the difference between the two numbers. Tell the children to show the answer on a number fan. Select one child to describe how they worked out the answer.

● Repeat for different pairs of numbers and select different less able children to explain the answer each time.

Potential difficulties	Further support
Children are unable to calculate the difference by counting on mentally.	Arrange, for example, 15 pennies and 20 pennies in rows. Count how many more, 'extra' pennies are in the row of 20.

Moving On
● Help children to relate 'finding the difference' to subtracting, by asking them to write a subtraction sentence beneath each picture, for example:
20p - 15p = 5p.

Shopkeeper's change

◼ What's the difference?

Nearest ten

Learning objective
(Y1) Count on and back in tens from and back to 0.

Mental starter
See the starter 30 on page 20.

You will need
Photocopiable page 77 per child, plus an enlarged A3 copy; counters; five A3 sheets of paper - numbered 10, 20, 30, 40, 50; 1–50 number cards, a highlighter pen.

Whole class work

● Display the enlarged photocopiable. Highlight the tens numbers on the number track. Tell the class that these numbers (which all end in zero) are called multiples of 10. Explain that this is because all of these numbers are made up of whole tens and no units.

● Place a counter on 28 on the track. Ask the children to imagine that the multiples of 10 are stations on a railway track and that the counter is a train travelling along the track. Ask: *Which two stations is the train between? Which station is it nearest to?*

● Demonstrate how to count on from 28 to 30 and back from 28 to 20 to confirm that 30 is the nearest 10 to 28.

● Repeat the activity with other numbers. Explain that if a number ends in 5 the train is an equal distance between stations so carries on to the next one.

Group work

● Give each child a copy of photocopiable page 77 and a counter. Stick the five A3 sheets of paper on the board to represent each of the train stations.

● Ask the children to place a counter on number 16. Ask them to work out which of the 'tens stations' the number lies between and which station it is nearest to. Can they explain how they worked it out? If necessary model again how to count on and back to calculate how far the train is from each 'station'.

● Select a child to write the number on the correct A3 sheet. Repeat this with several other numbers.

● Finally, give each child a number card. Ask them to work out which station the number is closest to and then write the number on the correct sheet. Repeat with other numbers.

Plenary

● Select children to spot the tens numbers on a class number line and circle them. Read out a number and ask them to shout out which tens number station it is nearest to. Target struggling children to see if they can answer correctly. Check the answers with a number line.

Potential difficulties	Further support
Children are not confident working with numbers up to 50.	Adapt the photocopiable so that it shows just one section of track such as 10 to 20. Use a set of 11-19 number cards.

Moving On
● Mentally round numbers to the nearest 10 without referring to any number lines or tracks.
● Investigate rounding numbers ending in a 9 to the nearest 10. *What do you notice? Which other numbers always round up to the next 10?*

Name _____

Nearest ten

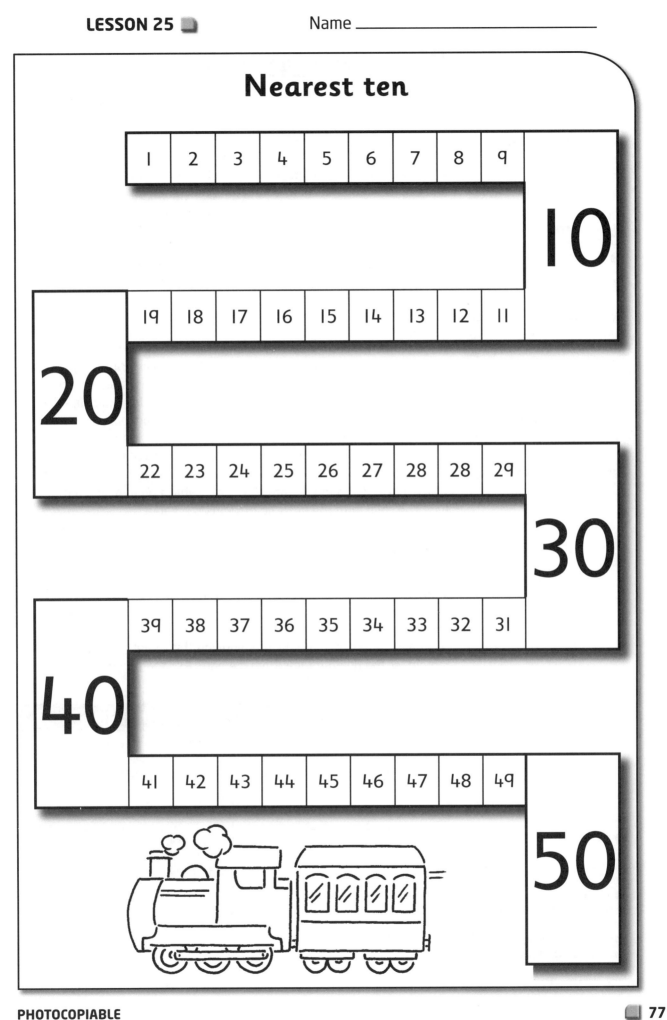

1	2	3	4	5	6	7	8	9

10

19	18	17	16	15	14	13	12	11

20

22	23	24	25	26	27	28	28	29

30

39	38	37	36	35	34	33	32	31

40

41	42	43	44	45	46	47	48	49

50

That's magic! (1)

Learning objective
(Y1) Know by heart all pairs of numbers with a total of 10.

Mental starter
See the starter, 37 on page 23.

You will need
A set of cards from photocopiable pages 79 and 81, 'That's magic 1' and 'That's magic 2' for each group; an enlarged copy of each set of cards; ten cardboard stars; Blu-Tack; paperclips; cubes and counters.

Whole class work

● Stick the enlarged sets of cards on the board. Tell the children that they are going to learn pairs of numbers that make a total of 10.
● Draw a large hat and magic wand on the board. Give a child 10 stars and ask them to stick them on the hat and wand.
● Discuss the arrangement of the stars, for example: *There are 4 stars on the hat and 6 stars on the wand – that makes 10 stars altogether.*
● Write the number fact 4 + 6 = 10 on the board. Ask a child to locate the two picture cards from the board which show this.
● Repeat until the class has found all the possible combinations of pairs of numbers that total 10.

Group work

● Teach the group to play 'How many stars?'. Use paperclips to join pairs of cards that total 10 together, put the 'clipped' pairs into a bag.
● Now remind the children that there is a total of 10 stars on each pair of cards. Pull a pair of cards out of the bag, saying, for example – *There are 4 stars coming out of the wand. How many stars are coming out of the top hat?* Whoever calls out the correct answer first scores a point.
● While the game is in progress provide targeted support for any children who you observe having difficulty calculating pairs of numbers which make 10. Continue until all the cards have been pulled out of the bag. The child with the most points wins the game.
● Repeat the game with the winner of the previous game becoming the 'magician' and asking the questions.

Plenary

● Write a missing number sentence on the board such as 5 + ? = 10. Ask the group to shout out the missing number. Repeat for other missing number problems which total 10.
● Finally, target specific children who you think might be struggling to remember the number facts from memory. Ask them to describe how they could work out the answer on their fingers.

Potential difficulties	Further support
Children find it difficult to make the link between their 10 fingers and the stars coming out of the top hats/ wands.	Explore number partners for 10 using concrete apparatus such as bead strings and cubes.
There is a large range of ability in the group.	Ask children to show their answers on a number fan. This will give those who take longer to calculate the answer more incentive to join in.

Moving On
● Use the wand and top-hat cards to play Snap or Pairs to help children learn by heart pairs of numbers that total 10.

That's magic (1)

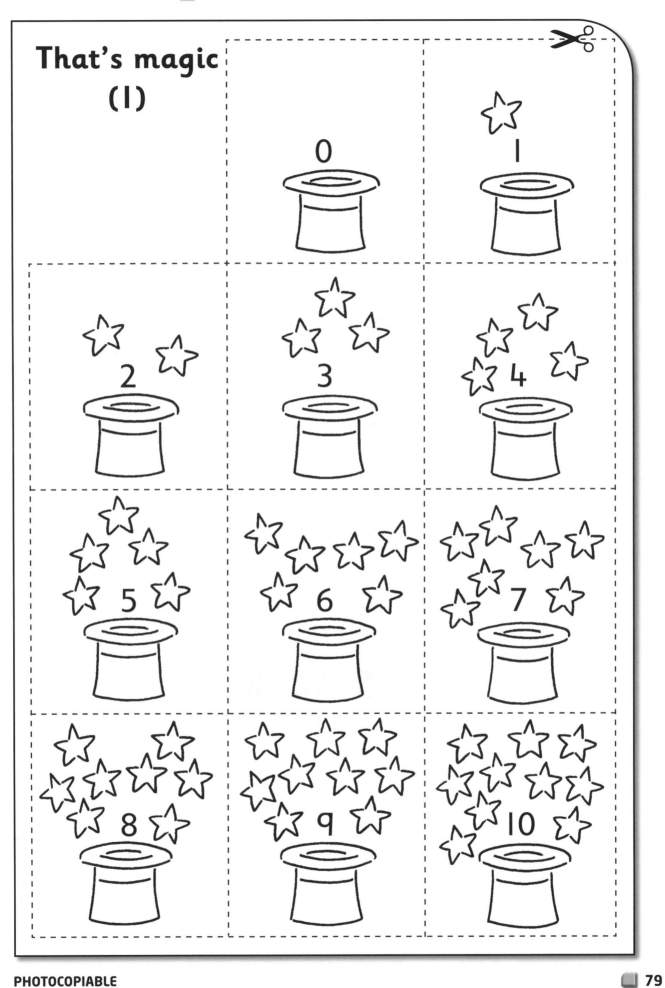

That's magic! (2)

Learning objective
(Y1) Know by heart all pairs of numbers with a total of 10.

Mental starter
See the starter 42 on page 24.

You will need
A set of enlarged cards from 'That's Magic (1)' and 'That's Magic (2)' (photocopiable pages 79 and 81) plus several sets for group work; paperclips; a magic wand with 4 stars on; a magician's hat with 6 stars on.

Whole class work
● Greet the children in role as a magician, ensure that the children cannot see your wand.
● Tell the children that the stars on your hat and wand always total 10. Ask: *How many stars are on my hat? How many stars will be on my magic wand?*
● Encourage the children to calculate the answer on their fingers. Reveal the wand. Count the total number of stars on the hat and wand to confirm that there are 10 altogether.
● Ask the children to suggest other hat and wand combinations.

Group work
● Tell the group that you are going show them an amazing magic trick! Spread a set of paper-clipped cards on the table. Remind the children that each pair of cards totals 10 (see 'That's Magic 1', page 78).
● Ask a child to point to a card. Explain that you are going to use your magic powers to read the number on the other side of the card. Wave your magic wand over the card, and 'guess' the number correctly. Repeat for other cards.
● Tell the group that you are going to teach them how to do the trick. Demonstrate how you are using your knowledge of number pairs to 10 to work out which number is on the reverse of the card. Model how you count on from the number on the front of the card until you reach 10. Put up a finger to represent each number name you say.
● Give the children the opportunity to practise the magic trick in pairs. Provide concrete apparatus to differentiate the activity for any children who find it difficult to calculate the number pairs by counting on.

Plenary
● Ask the less able group to tell you, from memory, pairs of numbers that total 10. Write these on the board (even if some of them are incorrect) and then, as a group, check if they are correct using the enlarged set of cards.

Potential difficulties	Further support
Children are unable to count on to find out how many more are needed to make a given total.	Provide practical apparatus such as a bead string or cubes.
Children need more visual reinforcement.	Demonstrate on a number line. For example: *There are 6 stars on the top hat. If I jump on 7, 8, 9, 10, that is 4 jumps. So there must be 4 stars on the wand.*

Moving On
● Use a similar lesson to motivate children to learn pairs of numbers with a total of 20.
● Use the cards to play games to develop quick recall of number pairs of 10.

That's magic (2)

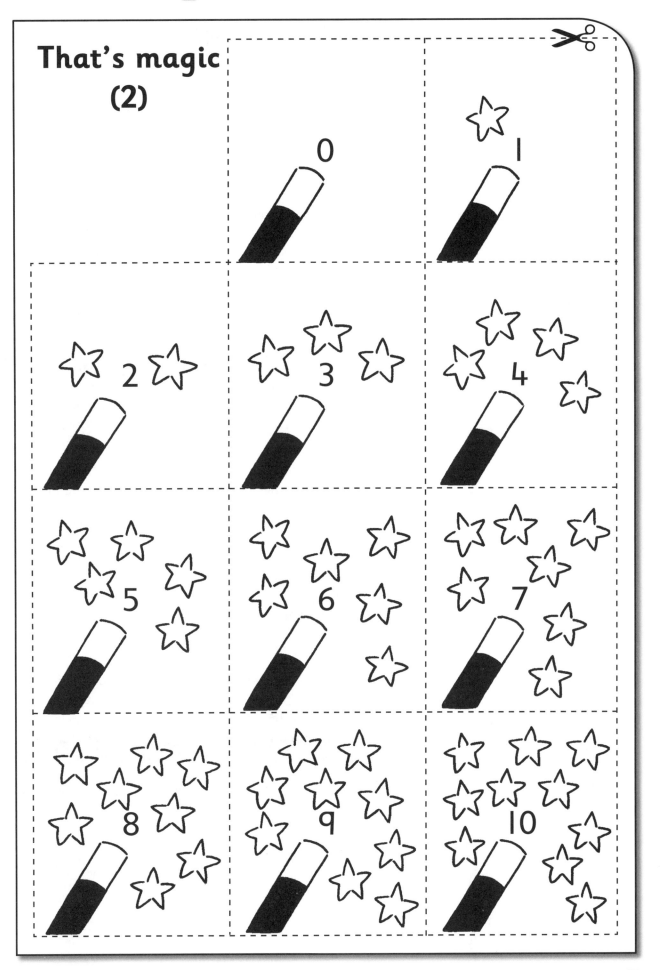

Ladybird doubles

Learning objective
(Y1) Know by heart addition doubles of all numbers to at least 5.

Mental starter
See the starter 7 on page 12.

You will need
Several copies of photocopiable page 83; a set of 7 cards made from the photocopiable page – 1 blank, 5 half-completed ladybirds and one ladybird with 4 spots drawn on each wing, folded in half and fastened with a paperclip; a set of 1-10 number cards in a bag; mirrors; felt-tipped pens; paper.

Whole class work

● Hold up the folded ladybird card. Ask the children to count the spots on each wing (without opening it up). Explain that because the ladybird has an equal number of spots on each wing it is called a *double*.
● Tell the children to close their eyes and imagine the whole ladybird. How many spots do they think it has altogether?
● Demonstrate how to use a mirror to create an image of the whole ladybird. Unfold the ladybird and count the spots together.
● Ask the children to hold up the appropriate number of fingers on each hand to represent the double number. Say together, *Double 4 makes 8 altogether*.

Paired work

● Give out a set of ladybird cards to each pair of children in the less able group. Ask the children to try and work out how many spots their ladybird has altogether when doubled.
● Let the children use the mirrors to view the complete ladybird and then draw on the missing spots. Hold up each of the completed ladybirds in front of the children and say the doubles number sentences together while the children hold up the appropriate number of fingers.

Group work

● Play 'Doubles Bingo'. Give each child a sheet of paper. Tell the children to pick four of the following numbers (0, 2, 4, 6, 8, 10) and write them down.
● Pick a number card from the bag and read it aloud, for example, say: *Double 5*. Anyone who has written the number 10 on their board may cross it out.
● Encourage the children who cannot recall the doubles to use their fingers to calculate the total.
● The winner is the first person to cross out all their numbers and shout *LADYBIRD!*

Plenary

● Give each child a set of number cards 2, 4, 6, 8, 10. Show different ladybird cards for the children to double. See how quickly the children can hold up the correct number card.

Moving On
● Learn addition doubles for the numbers 6 to 10.
● Begin to understand halving as the inverse of doubling. *If a ladybird double has 4 spots altogether, how many spots will there be on each wing?*

Potential difficulties	Further support
Children do not recognise a double as two numbers the same.	Play simple dice/dominoes games - have another turn if you shake/lay a double.
Children have difficulty committing the number facts to memory.	Use a range of activities to teach doubles facts, such as chanting doubles, using fingers or practical apparatus to double small numbers.

Ladybird doubles

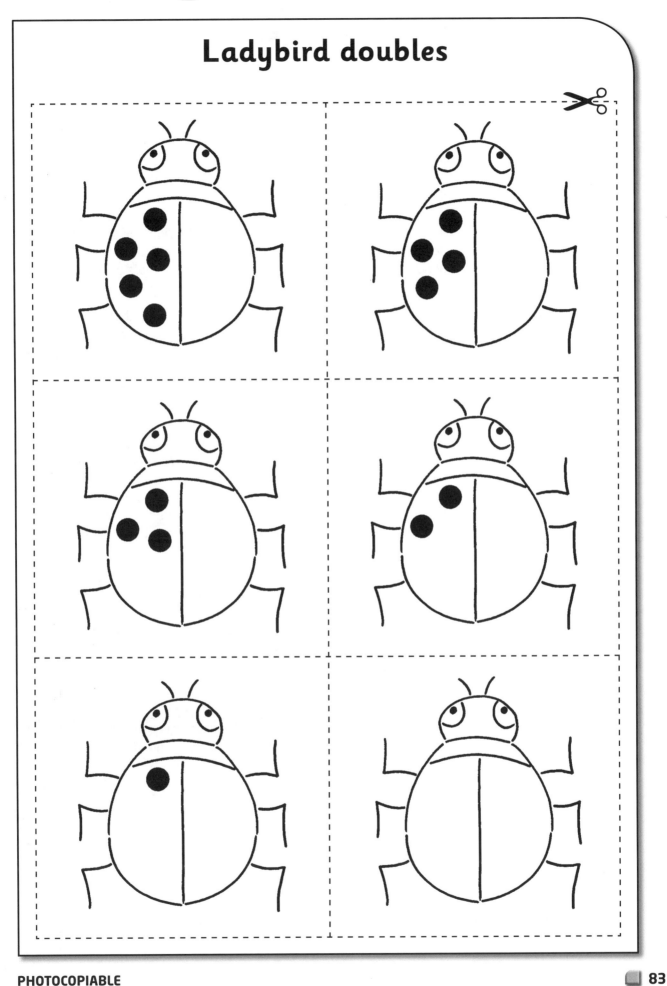

Double decker

Learning objective
(Y1) Know by heart addition doubles of all numbers to at least 5.

Mental starter
See the starter 19 on page 16.

You will need
A set of 'Double decker bus cards' from photocopiable page 85 per pair plus an enlarged set of cards for demonstration.

Whole class work

● Stick the 'Double decker bus cards' on the board. Discuss with the class why they are called 'Double decker' buses.
● Ask the children to count the number of passengers on each bus and to try and identify what all the buses have in common (they have the same number of passengers on each deck; the bus with no passengers in it represents double zero is zero).
● Focus on the bus with eight passengers. Explain that because it has 4 passengers on each deck it is called the 'Double 4 bus'. Ask: *Can you point to the Double 3 bus? How many people are on this bus altogether? What do you think the bus with 6 people on it is called?*

Group work

● Divide the less able learners into pairs to play 'Doubles'. Give each pair of children a set of cards (from photocopiable page 85). For each pair cut each of the buses in half and spread the cards out face down in two distinct piles.
● Ask the children, in their pairs, to take it in turns to turn over a card from each pile. If both cards have the same number of passengers on them the child shouts, *Double decker!*
● Next, bring the less able group back together and play a variation of the game to motivate them to learn doubles facts so that they can recall them quickly.
● Challenge the children to race to shout out the total number of passengers whenever a pair of doubles cards are turned over. The player who is first to call out the correct answer wins the pair.

Plenary

● Draw a bus stop on the board, write *Double 3* on it. Work with the less able group and ask: *Who can tell me how many people will be on this bus?*
● Encourage the group to use their fingers or mental imagery to work out the answer if they are unable to recall the number fact from memory. Repeat this with different numbers to assess if the children have understood the concept of doubling.

Potential difficulties	Further support
Children do not recognise a double as two numbers the same.	Give each child their own set of bus cards and play 'Show Me'. Draw the 'Double 3' bus stop. Ask the children to hold up the bus that they think will stop there.
Children find it difficult to commit number facts to memory.	Focus on one number fact for a whole session, such as double 4. Present the fact in different ways: use fingers, cubes, imagery and simple rhymes (such as, Double 4 is 8 biscuits on a plate!).

Moving On
● Introduce addition doubles for the numbers 6 to 10.

Double decker

Five little fish

Learning objectives
(Y1) Begin to know addition facts for all pairs of numbers with a total up to at least 10, and the corresponding subtraction facts.
(Y1) Know by heart addition facts for all pairs of numbers with a total up to at least 5.

Mental starter
See the starter 6 on page 11.

You will need
Several sets of numbered fish cards cut out from copies of photocopiable page 87; 5 small fish and a large shark cut out of thin card.

Whole class work
● Draw two goldfish bowls on the board. Explain that you would like the group to help you find pairs of numbers that total 5.
● Stick the five card fish in the first bowl. Write 5 + 0 = 5. Model how to find all the pairs of numbers that total five by systematically moving the fish into the second bowl, one at a time.
● Write all the number pairs in a list on the board: 5 + 0; 4 + 1 and so on. Read the list of number sentences together.

Group work
● Organise the group so that they are sitting in a circle on the floor. Place the five cardboard fish and the shark in the centre of the circle.
● Tell the children that you would like them to solve some simple problems using their knowledge of pairs of numbers that make 5. Ask them to close their eyes. Hide 2 fish underneath the shark. Ask: *How many fish were there altogether? How many can you see now? How many fish has the shark eaten?*
● Show the children how to work out the answer using the fingers on one hand to represent the 5 fish. Repeat the activity with different numbers of fish.
● Split the children into two smaller groups to play a pairing game. Give each group two sets of fish cards 1–5 (from photocopiable page 87). Write the numbers on the back of each card. Instruct the children to spread the cards out number-side-up on the table.
● Tell the children to take it in turns to take two numbers that they think total 5. Let them count the total number of fish on the other side of the cards to check. If they have made a pair they may keep the cards otherwise they should be returned to the table. The winner is the player who collects the most pairs.

Plenary
● Call out a number from 0 to 5. Ask the children to use their fingers to show you the number needed to add on to make 5.

Potential difficulties	Further support
Children cannot commit number facts to memory.	Reinforce number pairs that make five with a variety of concrete apparatus such as bead strings, cubes and dominoes.

Moving On
● Ask the children to investigate and learn pairs of numbers that make 8.
● Practise rapid recall of pairs of numbers that make 5 in a range of contexts, such as playing Snap or Bingo.

Five little fish

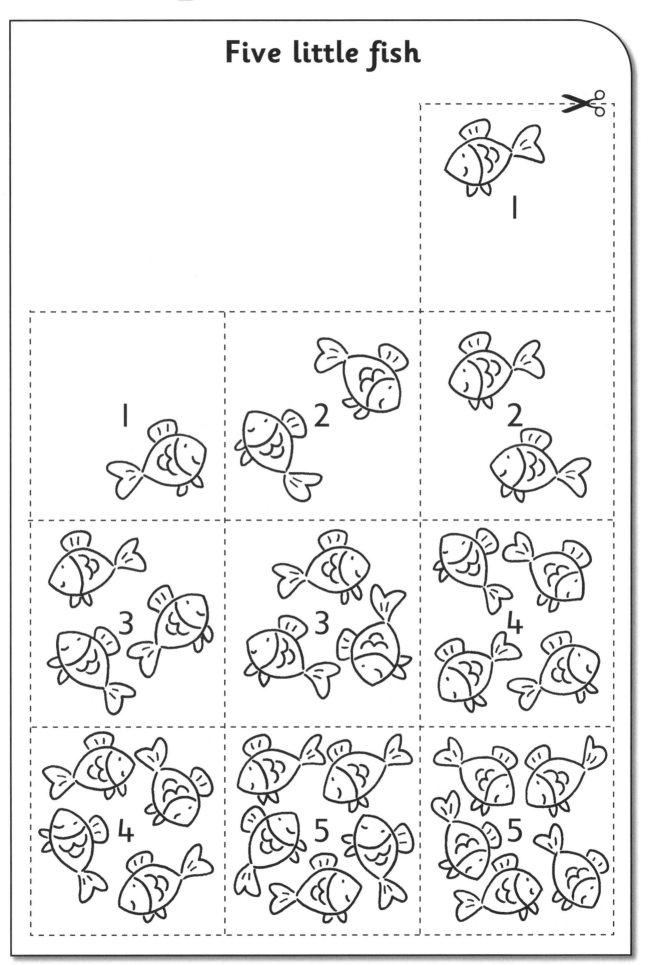

Near doubles

Whole class work
- Ask the children to explain what a double is? Ask: *If I double a number what do I do to it?*
- Teach the class how to add a near double, for example, 4 + 5, by doubling one of the numbers and then adjusting by 1.
- Set some problems for the children to answer and select specific children to describe how they added two numbers using the near doubles strategy. Ask them how they knew whether to add or take away 1.

Group work
- Spread a set of dominoes face-up on the table. Ask the group to identify all the doubles dominoes and to say the total number of spots on each one.
- Hold up the domino with 4 spots on one side and 3 on the other. Model how to calculate the total number of spots on the domino in two steps. First show double 3. Then lift your finger to reveal the extra spot. Count on 1 more to find the total number of spots on the domino.
- Finally, hold up other near doubles dominoes. Let each child in the group have a turn at covering a spot on one of the dominoes to make it look like a double. Ask them to work out the total number of spots on the domino using the two-step method you have demonstrated.

Independent work
- Give each child in the group two 1-6 dice and a copy of photocopiable page 89. Tell the children to roll both dice together. If the two numbers rolled make a near double, tell the children to draw the dice on their sheet and add up the total number of spots.
- Talk to the children about what they are doing. Check that all the children understand how they can use their knowledge of doubles to help them add near doubles.

Plenary
- Give each child in the group a number fan.
- Write different near doubles on the board. Ask the children to add the two numbers together as quickly as they can and show the answer on their number fan.
- Select specific children to explain how they used their knowledge of doubles facts to calculate a near double.

Potential difficulties	Further support
Children cannot recall doubles facts mentally.	Play doubling Snap, Bingo or Pairs to provide opportunities for children to practise recalling doubles facts from memory.

Near doubles

■ Roll two dice.

■ If you roll a near double draw the dice and add up the total number of spots.

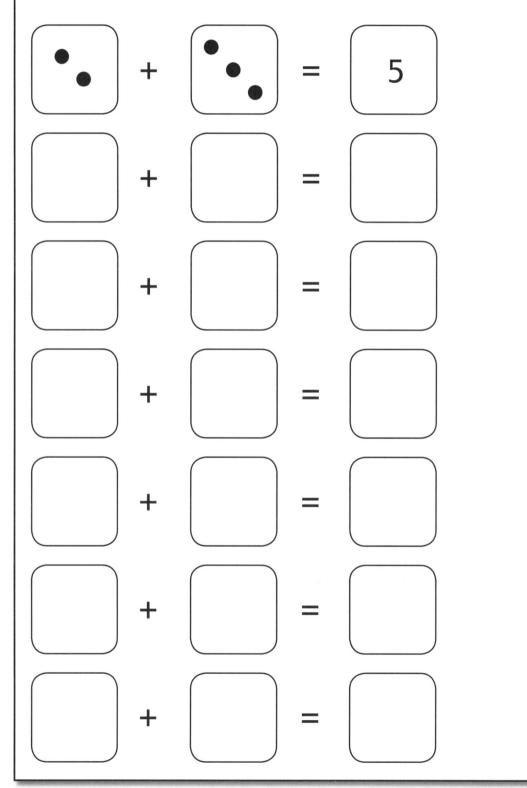

Take me home

Learning objectives
(Y2) Know by heart all pairs of numbers that total 20.
(Y2) Extend understanding of the operations of addition and subtraction.

Mental starter
See the starter 35 on page 22.

You will need
Photocopiable page 91 (one copy for Group work and one for each child in Independent work); a large 1-20 number track; 4 small toys; counters and a bead string (20).

Whole class work

● Ask a child to partition the beads on the bead string into two groups and say an addition number statement to reflect what they have done (such as, *15 add 5 makes 20*).
● Say: *If 15 add 5 is 20 what is 20 subtract 5?* As you say this, move the beads on the bead string to illustrate that subtracting 5 'undoes' adding 5.
● Repeat this activity several times. Move the beads on the string each time to emphasise that addition and subtraction are inverse operations and that subtracting a number 'undoes' adding that number.

Group work

● Place a toy on number 20 (home) on the number track on photocopiable page 91. Put the other toys on numbers 11, 13, 15.
● Explain that the toy (at home) wants to visit his friend at number 13. Ask the less able group to count as you move the toy back along the track to 13. Ask: *How many steps did the toy take? How many steps will it need to take to get back home?* Take the toy to visit his other friends in the same way.
● Draw a 'Take me home' number circle on the board, copied from the photocopiable. Write 20 in the top box and 19 in the bottom box. Choose a child to move the toy back to 19 on the number track. Count the number of steps. Write *-1* in the left-hand box. Ask the group how many steps they think the toy will have to take to get back to 20. Check and then write *+1* in the right-hand box.
● Discuss what the group notice about the two numbers. Why are they the same?

Independent work

● Give each child a copy of the photocopiable page and a toy (or counter). Ask the children to fill in the missing numbers in each number circle (using the toy as a counter to help them).

Plenary

● Tell the less able group to count as you move the toy from 20 back to 9 on the large track. Select a child to say how many steps the toy will need to take to get home again. Repeat with different numbers.

Potential difficulties	Further support
Children do not realise that adding 3 undoes subtracting 3.	Reinforce this concept in other practical contexts. For example, say: *I have 20 cubes, I'll give you 3 of them. Give me the 3 cubes back. How many have I got now?*

Moving On
● Give children number statements to sort into pairs involving inverses.

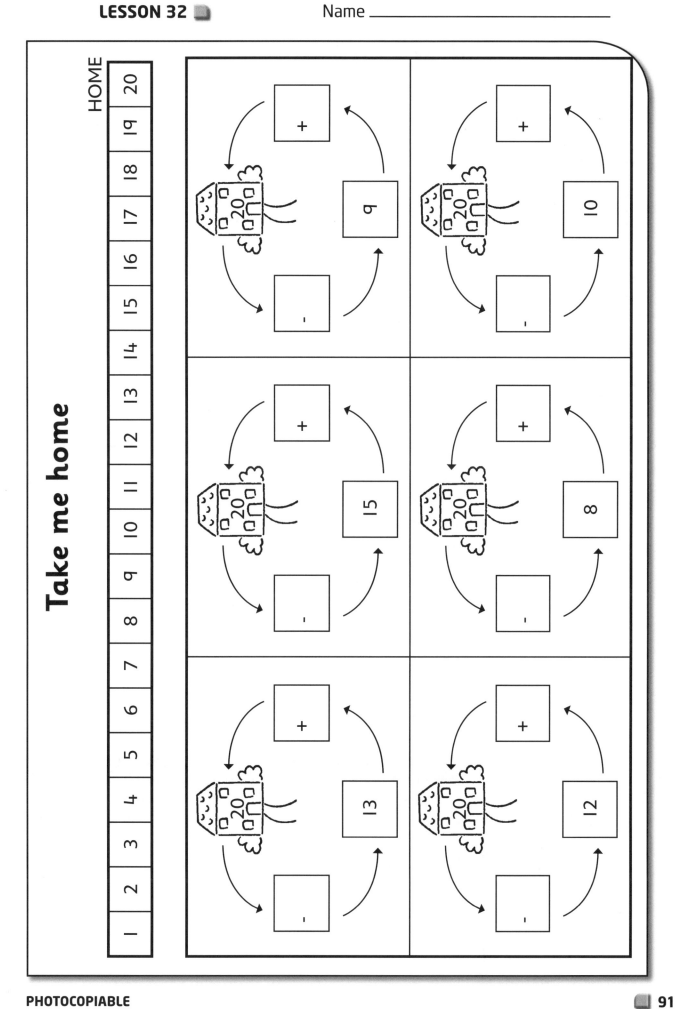

Take me home

1	2	3	4	5	6	7	8	9	10	11	12	13	14	15	16	17	18	19	20

HOME

Back to ten

Learning objectives
(Y2) To understand that subtraction is the inverse of addition.
(Y2) State the subtraction corresponding to a given addition, and vice versa.

Mental starter
See the starter 47 on page 26.

You will need
A laminated copy of photocopiable page 93; whiteboard pens/markers; card and 10 'cow' cards per pair; sheets of green card (fields); bead string (10 beads).

Whole class work

● Tell the class that they are going to be learning about the relationship between addition and subtraction.
● Ask the children to think of four different addition/subtraction number sentences relating to the numbers 10, 3 and 7. Write the number sentences on the board. Represent visually that subtraction is the opposite of addition by moving beads on a bead string. For example, *10 - 3 = 7 so we know that 7 + 3 makes 10.*
● Invite individuals to join the corresponding addition and subtraction facts on the board.

Group work

● Place the 10 cow cards in a 'field'. Explain that some of the cows are going to escape and that you would like the children to help you get all ten cows back in the field.
● Choose a volunteer to move the cows as you tell a story. For example: *Farmer Sally had 10 cows in her field. One day 4 of the cows escaped.* Ask another child to record this as a number sentence (10 - 4 = 6).
● Now ask the group to say what the farmer needs to do to get all 10 cows back in the field. Do they need to add animals or take some away? Write the corresponding number sentence (6 + 4 = 10).
● Compare the two number sentences and identify and describe the similarities and differences. Repeat the activity with different numbers.

Paired work

● Give pairs of children a laminated 'Back to ten' card, 10 cow cards and a 'field'. Ask the children to make up their own stories. One child should begin the story and remove a number of the cows from the field. The second child should finish the story by getting the 10 cows back in the field.
● Help the children to record their stories as number sentences on their laminated 'Back to ten' cards.

Plenary

● Pick different children from the group to tell a farmyard number story. Ask the rest of the group to identify the subtraction which has taken place and state the inverse addition.

Moving On
● Ask children to work independently to make as many addition and subtraction facts as they can using, for example: 4, 6, 10, -, +, =.
● Pose questions such as *If 20 - 5 = 15 what is 15 + 5?* Ask children to answer the questions without the aid of apparatus.

Potential difficulties	Further support
Children do not recognise that adding 5 undoes subtracting 5.	Reinforce this concept in other contexts, say: *Show me 10 fingers, take 3 away, how can you get back to 10?*

Back to ten

$$10 - \boxed{} = \boxed{}$$

$$\boxed{} + \boxed{} = 10$$

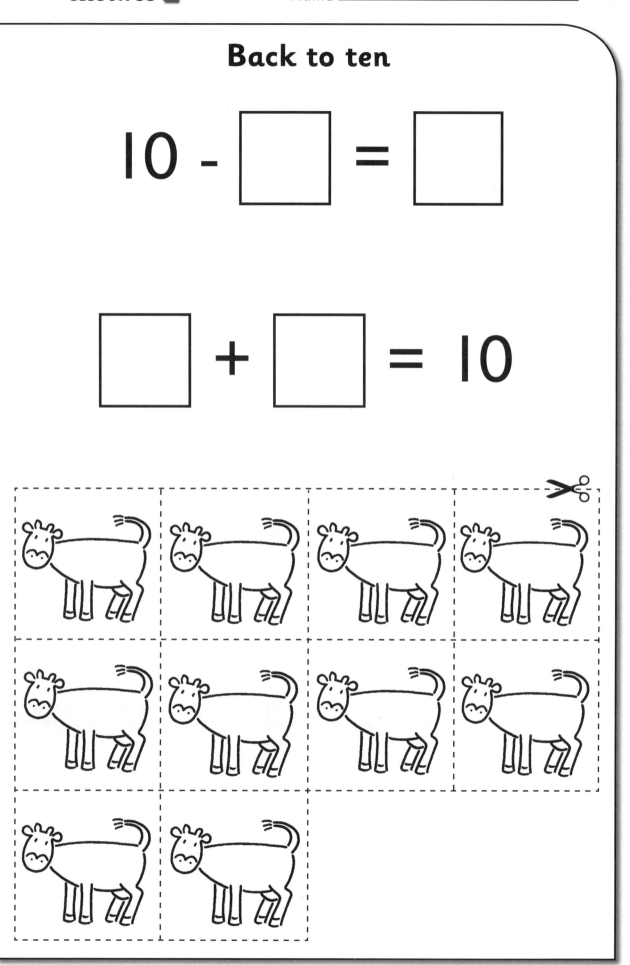

Adding 11

Whole class work

● Tell the class there is 45p in your purse. Hold up a 10p coin and then add it to the purse. Ask: *How much money is in the purse altogether?* Repeat, this time adding a 1p coin.
● Write 45 + 11 = 56 on the board to show the calculation. Encourage the children to recognise and explain how they used the strategies they already knew for adding 10 and 1 to a number to help them add 11.
● Add 11p to several other amounts.

Group work

● Ask one child in the group to count 4 pennies onto the purse card on the sheet. Place a 10p and a 1p coin on the 'Add 11p' box. Demonstrate how to add the 11p to the 4p already in the purse in two steps by first adding 10p and then 1p.
● Working together as a group add 11 to other small numbers of pennies in the purse. If children find it difficult to add 10 and 1 mentally, refer to the 100-square. Remind the group of the 'quick tricks' for adding 10 and 1 on a 100-square. (See the 'Swim to shore' lesson on page 38.)

Independent work

● Give each child a copy of photocopiable page 95. Ask them to put seven pennies in the purse and place a 10p and a 1p coin in the 'Add 11' box. Tell them to add 11p to the 7p already in the purse, using the two-step method you have shown them.
● Encourage them to complete all the examples on the sheet, supervise and assist the children where necessary.

Plenary

● Circle a number on the 100-square. Tell the children to add 11 to the number as quickly as they can.
● Select a child to circle the answer and explain how they worked it out. Repeat with different numbers.
● Encourage the group to notice and describe the pattern that is created on the 100-square.

Potential difficulties	Further support
Children cannot say the number that is 1 or 10 more than a given number.	Have individual 100-squares available for children to refer to.
Children calculate the answer by counting up all the coins instead of counting on 10 and then 1.	Make the children add 10p and tell you how much money is in the purse before they add 1p.

Adding 11

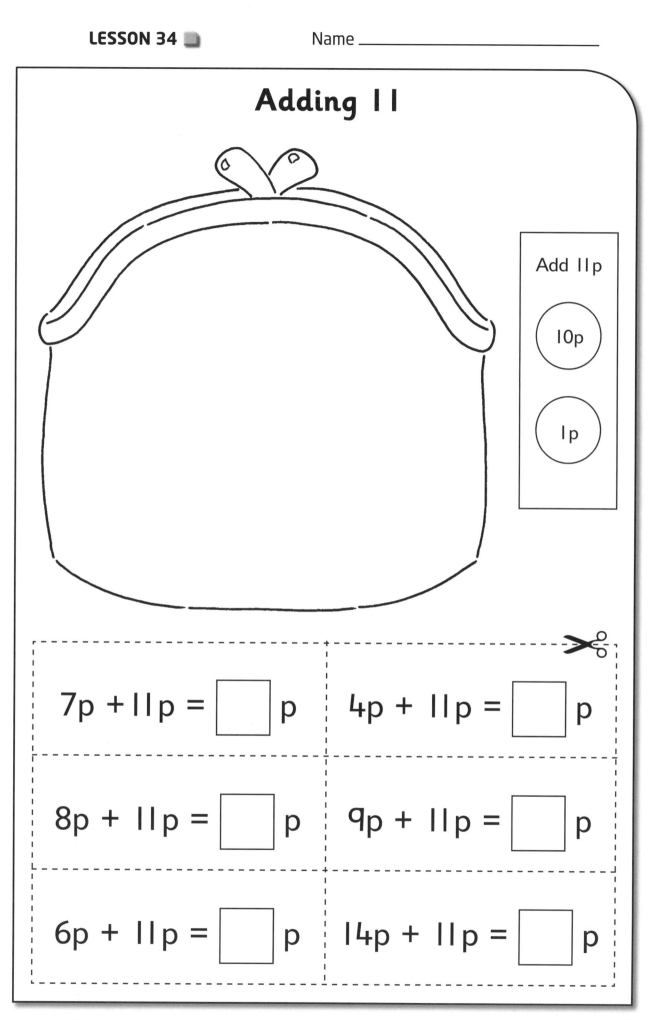

Add 11p

10p

1p

7p + 11p = ☐ p   4p + 11p = ☐ p

8p + 11p = ☐ p   9p + 11p = ☐ p

6p + 11p = ☐ p   14p + 11p = ☐ p

Five and a bit

Learning objective
(Y1) Begin to partition into '5 and a bit' when adding 6, 7, 8 or 9, then recombine (eg 6 + 8 = 5 + 1 + 5 + 3 = 10 + 4 = 14).

Mental starter
See the starter 32 on page 21.

You will need
Photocopiable page 97; eight counters; number cards 6, 7, 8, 9 for each child in the less able group.

Whole class work

● Write 9 + 7 on the board. Explain that you are going to work out the total by first breaking the two numbers into 'five and a bit' and then adding all the smaller numbers together.
● Invite the children to hold up 9 fingers. Ask one child to describe how many fingers they are holding up on each hand. Write 5 + 4 on the board.
● Ask the class to hold up 7 fingers. Pick a child to describe how they have partitioned 7 into 'five and a bit'. Write 5 + 2 on the board.
● Demonstrate how to add 9 + 7 by recombining the four smaller numbers that you have partitioned them into:
5 + 5 = 10; 4 + 2 = 6; 10 + 6 = 16.
● Repeat this activity for other number sentences.

Group work

● Ask the group to hold up 9 fingers. Ask one child to say how many fingers they are holding up on each hand. Write 5 + 4 on the board. Partition the numbers 6, 7 and 8 in the same way.
● Play 'Five and a bit' with the group – give each child a game board (photocopiable page 97) and some counters. Shuffle the number cards and place them face down in a pile in the middle of the table.
● Ask a child to turn over a number card, partition the number into 'five and a bit' and then cover the correct star or planet box on the sheet.
● Encourage the children to use their fingers to help them partition the number.
● Take it in turns until the winner has covered all the stars and planets.

Plenary

● Hold up one of the digit cards. Select individuals to say how the numbers can be partitioned into 'five and a bit'.
● Write the number sentence 6 + 8 = 14 on the board. Select a child to explain the process of partitioning and recombining numbers to calculate the answer.

Potential difficulties	Further support
Children need a more visual representation of the process of partitioning and recombining.	Have sticks of 6, 7, 8, 9 Multilink cubes available. Ask the children to split the towers of cubes into 'five and a bit' and then recombine.
Children find it difficult to partition two numbers into 'five and a bit' and then recombine.	Use number sentences that only require children to partition one number such as 5 + 8.

Moving On
● Teach children to add two-digit numbers by partitioning into tens and ones and recombining.

Five and a bit

5 and 3

5 and 1

5 and 2

5 and 2

5 and 4

5 and 3

5 and 1

5 and 4

Afternoon tea

Learning objectives
(Y1) Solve simple word problems set in 'real life' contexts
(Y1) Explain methods and reasoning orally.
(Y1) Choose and use appropriate number operations to solve problems.

Mental starter
See the starter 24 on page 18.

You will need
Photocopiable page 99 (copy and cut out a set of cakes for each child in the less able group; a laminated set of cake cards for the whole class teaching activity and some paper plates.

Whole class work
● Stick the cake cards and a paper plate on the board. Tell a simple number story. For example: *There were 8 cakes on a plate. Sam ate 2 of the cakes. How many cakes were left on the plate?*
● Pick a child to act out the story using the cake cards and ask the following questions: *How many cakes were on the plate at the beginning of the story? Sam ate 2 of the cakes, do you need to add 2 more cakes or take 2 cakes away? How many cakes are left on the plate?*
● Set another problem, for example: *Mandeep had 5 cakes. Her sister Geeta had 4 cakes. How many cakes did Mandeep and Geeta have altogether?* Choose children to act the problem out, encouraging them to explain their methods orally.

Group work
● Give each child in the less able group a set of cake cards and a plate.
● Pose 'story' problems for the group to solve practically. The abilities of the children in the group will determine the complexity of the problems you set, the size of numbers involved and the operations needed to solve them.
● Ask different children to explain and demonstrate how they were able to solve each problem. What words did they hear that helped them to know whether to add or take cakes away?
● Ask each of the children to make up a number story of their own for another person in the group to solve.

Plenary
● Ask the children in the less able group to close their eyes. Tell a simple number story. Encourage them to use mental imagery to solve the problem.
● Let the children check the answer using the cake cards.

Potential difficulties	Further support
Children have difficulty making up their own number stories.	Make up number stories as a group activity. Ask: *Who will the story be about? How many cakes do they have? Are they going to take more cakes or eat some? How many?*
Children have difficulty working out which operation is needed to solve a problem.	Focus on one type of problem such as subtraction. Introduce a variety of mathematical language and help the children to relate these words and phrases to the operation of subtraction.

Moving On
● Set more complex problems using larger numbers.
● Ask the children to record, in their own way, how they solved a problem.
● Tell 'story' problems that require children to combine two different operations.

Afternoon tea

Money bags

Learning objective
(Y2) Recognise all coins.

Mental starter
See the starter 30 on page 20.

You will need
A copy of photocopiable page 101 per child; a 1p, 2p, 5p, 10p, 20p, 50p, £1 and £2 coin for each child in the group.

Group work
● Give all the children in the group a copy of photocopiable page 101 and a set of coins. Allow everyone a few moments to match each coin into the correct space on the sheet.
● Hold up a 5p coin. Ask the children to find that coin in their 'money bag'. Invite individuals to say something they have noticed about the coin, such as: *It is made of metal. It has a number 5 on it.*
● Repeat for each of the coins in the money bag, helping the children to describe the colour, texture, shape and size.

Group work
● Demonstrate how to play 'Guess my coin' to the less able group. Tell the children to turn the coins on their 'money bag' so that the Queen's head is visible.
● Now describe one of the coins in detail and ask the children to listen carefully. For example: *I am thinking of a coin. It is large and silver and it has seven sides.* (50p)
● Invite the children to hold up the coin they think has all the properties you described. Ask them to tell you the value of the coin.

Paired work
● Organise the children so that they are sitting back to back with a partner. Let them carry on playing the game in pairs, taking it in turns to be the describer. Ask them to turn round and face each other when the child doing the guessing holds up their guess (a coin).
● Work alongside any children you have identified as having difficulty understanding or using appropriate language to describe coin properties.

Plenary
● Play 'Show Me the Coin!' with the less able learners. Check that everyone has their coins turned so that the values are concealed.
● Name a coin such as a 20p. Ask the children to hold up the coin they think you have named without turning the coins over to look at the numbers.
● The first child to hold up the correct coin becomes the caller and names a different coin for the rest of the group to find.
● Make a note of any children who are holding up the wrong coins - you may need to revise the coin recognition with them again.

Potential difficulties	Further support
Children find it difficult to recognise and name all the different coins.	Focus on the properties and names of fewer coins at once.
Children confuse £1/1p or £2/2p coins.	Sort pennies and pound coins into labelled money bags. Set up a penny/pound shop in the classroom where all items cost £1 or 1p.

Moving On
● Develop children's appreciation of the value of the different coins. For example, asking which is worth more or less.
● Introduce pound and pence notation.

Money bags

At the café

Learning objectives
(Y1) Solve simple problems set in money contexts.
(Y2) Use knowledge that addition can be done in any order to do mental calculations more efficiently.
(Y2) Put the larger number first and count on in ones.

Mental starter
See the starter 41 on page 24.

You will need
A copy of photocopiable page 103 for each pair of children plus an enlarged copy; small pots containing a mixture of 1p, 2p, 5p and 10p coins.

Whole class work
● Put an enlarged copy of the café menu on the board. Invite one child to order a drink and snack from the menu. Note the price of each item on the board (for example, 3p; 8p).
● Ask the class, in pairs or individually, to calculate the customer's bill and then explain how they worked out the answer (for example, counting on from 1; counting on from a number; or by putting the largest number first and counting on).
● Consider which of the methods described is the most efficient way of adding the two numbers.
● Model how to calculate a different customer's bill using the strategy of counting on from the larger number. Ask the class to calculate other customers' bills using this strategy.

Paired work
● Organise the less able children to work in pairs – one as a waiter/waitress and the other a customer. Instruct the children to swap roles after each transaction.
● Give each pair of children a pot of coins and a menu. Tell the customers to place an order for a drink and a snack.
● The waiter/waitress jots the two prices down in their notebook, works out the total cost of the two items and then writes out a bill. The customer counts out the correct amount of money to pay.
● Listen and observe as the children are engaged in the activity. Support individual children by further modelling the strategy of counting on from the larger number to find the total. Suggest that the waiter/waitress records the cost of the highest priced item first to make this easier.

Plenary
● Order a drink and two snacks from the menu. Ask the less able children to calculate the total cost as quickly as they can and then demonstrate their method.
● Can they explain why it is sensible to count on from the largest number? Provide support and assistance for those who are struggling.

Potential difficulties	Further support
Children are unable to find a total by counting on, because they are unsure of the next number in the number sequence.	Have number tracks available. Demonstrate how to count on from the larger number.
Children have difficulty making an exact amount using smaller coins.	Limit the coins available to 10p and 1p coins.

Moving On
● Adjust the price of the drinks on the menu to amounts beyond 20p to give children some practice at counting on from larger numbers.

At the café

Menu

hot chocolate 10p

coffee 9p

tea 8p

milk 11p

milkshake 14p

lemonade 12p

apple juice 13p

orange juice 10p

chocolate bar 4p

sweets 2p

biscuit 3p

ice-cream 6p

cake 4p

apple 5p

Change machine

Learning objective
(Y1) Solve simple problems set in 'real life', money or measurement contexts.
(Y1) Explain methods and reasoning orally.
(Y1) Find totals and change from up to 20p.

Mental starter
See the starter 11 on page 13.

You will need
A copy of photocopiable page 105 for each child; a selection of small objects priced between 1p and 10p; several pots of 1p and several 10p coins.

Whole class work

● Pretend to be a shopkeeper. Display the items you have for sale in your shop.
● Ask one child to come to the shop and choose an item they would like to buy. Tell them to pay for it using the 10p coin.
● Describe the transaction which takes place. For example, *Ellie wants to buy a pencil, it costs 7p but she has given the shopkeeper 10p.* Establish that the customer has given more money than the item costs so she needs some change (3p).
● Do the children know a strategy that will help them to work out how much change to give? Refer the children to a number line and show them how to count on from the product price to work out the change.
● Repeat the activity and choose different children to play the parts of the customer and the shopkeeper.

Group work

● Tell the less able children that they have a 'special' machine to help them work out how much change they need to give to a customer.
● Demonstrate how to use the 'change machine' photocopiable. Place ten 1p coins onto the spaces provided. Explain that these represent the 10p that the customer will pay with. Explain that because a pencil costs 7p the shopkeeper can keep 7 of the pennies (remove 7 pennies). Ask: *Can you see how many pennies are left?* Explain that you must give the customer the 3p because that is the change they are owed.

Paired work

● Divide the children into pairs. Choose one child in each pair to be the shopkeeper and give them a change machine sheet, some items to sell and a pot of pennies.
● Give the other child a 10p coin and ask them to buy an item from the shop and pay for it with their 10p coin. The shopkeeper then calculates and gives the correct change.

Plenary

● Give each child in the less able group a 'change machine' and some pennies. Set a problem, such as: *Abigail bought a toy that cost 5p. She gave the shopkeeper 10p. How much change did she get?* Ask different children to explain how they worked out the answer.

Potential difficulties	Further support
Children do not understand that one 10p coin is equivalent to ten 1p coins.	Provide opportunities for children to exchange 2p, 5p and 10p coins for the equivalent value in 1p coins.

Moving On
● Teach children how to work out change from 10p by counting on from the product's price.
● Set simple two-stepped problems - buy two items which total less than 10p and work out the change.

Change machine

■ Use the change machine to work out how much change to give the customer.

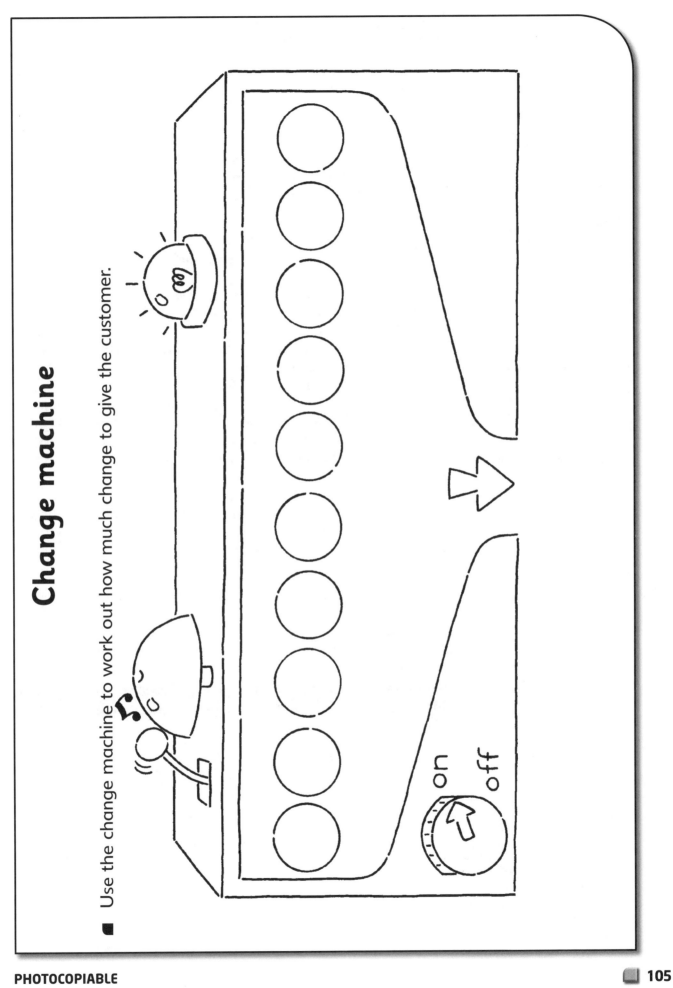

Stamp collector

Learning objectives
(Y1) Solve simple problems set in 'real life', money or measurement contexts.
(Y1) Explain methods and reasoning orally.

Mental starter
See the starter 48 on page 26.

You will need
Five copies of photocopiable page 107 (cut out the stamps and lay them out in piles on a desk); one set of stamps enlarged and coloured in; Blu-Tack; money pots containing a mixture of 1p and 2p coins.

Whole class work
● Stick the enlarged 'stamps' on the board. Give the children a few moments to look at them. Pose some simple questions such as: *How many stamps are there altogether? What does the number in the corner of each stamp mean?*
● Ask individuals to point to specific stamps, for example, the most or least expensive stamp.

Group work
● Sit behind the desk. Tell the children that you would like them to come to the 'post office' and buy some stamps to make their own stamp collection.
● Organise the children to work in pairs. Give each pair a pot of money. Hold up the stamp that costs 5p. Instruct the children to take 5p out of their pot to pay for the stamp. (Invite the confident children to explain how they made 5p using smaller coins.) Alternatively, model how to make 5p using the 1p and 2p coins.
● Let each pair come up and buy a 5p stamp.
● Next, tell each pair to make 8p using 1p and 2p coins from their pot.
● Encourage each pair to describe to the rest of the group which coins they have used. Count with the group to check that the coins total 8p, if they do, let the pair have the 8p stamp to add to their collection.
● Encourage the group to see that there is more than one way of making 8p using the coins available.
● Challenge each pair to buy as many of the different stamps as they can from your post office. Tell them to decide which stamp to buy, count out the exact amount, then come and buy it.

Plenary
● Investigate the different ways of paying for some of the stamps with the less able group.
● Select different children and record their explanations on the board so that the rest of the group can see and understand the various ways to pay using different coins.

Potential difficulties	Further support
Children have difficulty making an exact amount using smaller coins.	Spend longer modelling how to make different amounts. Demonstrate how to tap the 2p twice when calculating the total value of a set of 1p and 2p coins. Let struggling children begin by making amounts using just 1p coins and then exchanging two of the 1p coins for a 2p coin.

Moving On
● Increase the price of each stamp. Ask the children to count out the exact amount using a wider variety of coins.
● Set multi-stepped problems such as buying two stamps at once.

Stamp collector

Car 7p

Lorry 12p

White van 6p

Double decker bus 3p

Mini bus 10p

Train 11p

Moter bike 8p

Mountain bike 4p

Narow boat 5p

Coach 9p

Feeling fruity

Learning objectives
(Y1) Understand and use the vocabulary related to mass.
(Y1) Measure using uniform non-standard units.

Mental starter
See the starter 50 on page 27.

You will need
A copy of photocopiable page 109 per child in the less able group; one of each of the fruits pictured on the sheet; balancing scales; cubes; labels (heavier, lighter).

Whole class work
● Tell the children that they are going to investigate and compare the mass of some fruits. Talk about what the term 'mass' means.
● Pass two of the fruits around the class. Ask the children to consider which of the fruits feels heaviest/lightest.
● Place one fruit in each side of the balancing scales and discuss what happens. Ask: *Which fruit is heaviest/lightest? How do you know?* Repeat the activity with different combinations of the fruits.

Group work
● Play the heavier/lighter game.
● Give each child in the group cards labelled 'heavier' and 'lighter'. Stand in front of the group holding a lemon. Explain that you are going to name an object and that you would like the children to show whether they think it would be heavier or lighter than the lemon by holding up the relevant card.

Paired work
● Show children the selection of fruits. Explain that you would like them find out how many cubes are needed to balance each of the fruits and then use this information to work out which of the fruits is the heaviest.
● Demonstrate how to work out how many cubes are needed to balance the lemon on a balancing scale. Show the children how to record this by writing the appropriate number of cubes in the picture of the lemon on the photocopiable sheet.
● Divide the children into pairs and give each pair a balancing scale, cubes and a copy of photocopiable page 109. Tell the children to weigh each fruit in turn and record how many cubes are needed to balance it.
● Work alongside the children, encouraging them to discuss what they are doing, using the appropriate vocabulary. Ask targeted questions such as: *How many cubes did you need to balance the banana? Is it heavier or lighter than the lemon? How do you know?*

Plenary
● Revise the vocabulary that the children have been using such as *mass, heavier, lighter* and so on.
● Hold up a pencil and a book. Ask the group to predict which object they think is the heaviest and discuss how they could use the balance to check their prediction.

Moving On
● Show children how to measure and compare masses using standard units such as kilograms or grams.

Potential difficulties	Further support
Children are unable to interpret the data they have gathered.	Concentrate on comparing one fruit (such as the lemon) with each of the other fruits. Ask questions such as: *Which is heavier, the lemon or the banana? How can we check?*
The children do not weigh objects accurately.	Model the weighing process before each comparison.

Feeling fruity

◾ Write how many cubes balance each of the different fruits.

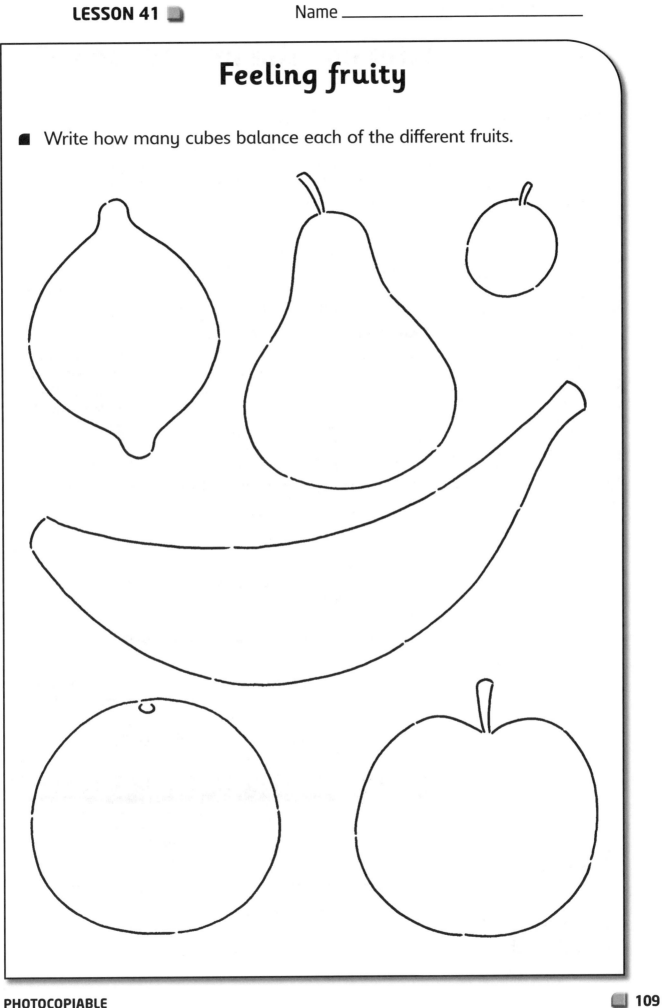

Who has the longest scarf?

Learning objectives
(Y1) Suggest suitable uniform non-standard units to estimate, then measure a length.
(Y1) Explain methods and reasoning orally.

Mental starter
See the starter 49 on page 27.

You will need
A copy of the vocabulary cards from photocopiable page 111; 6 scarves of different lengths; several toy animals each with a strip of different coloured fabric tied round its neck like a scarf (all different lengths).

Whole class work

● Tell the children that they are going to investigate length. Give six children a scarf to wear. Read and display the vocabulary cards – 'longest' and 'shortest'. Discuss the meaning of the two words.
● Choose two children wearing scarves to stand up. Invite a child to guess which of the two scarves is the longest. Let them come and test their prediction. Model how to do this by laying the two scarves side by side to allow a direct comparison of their lengths to be made. Label the scarves longest and shortest.
● Repeat the activity choosing different children each time.
● Finally, lay all the scarves out on the floor. Compare the scarves and label the longest and the shortest.

Group work

● Put two toys on the table. Ask the children to suggest how they could find out which toy is wearing the longest scarf without making a direct comparison. Put a selection of uniform non-standard units (such as cubes and paperclips) out in front of the group to stimulate ideas.
● Discuss the children's ideas. Pick a child to measure a scarf using cubes or alternatively demonstrate how to do this yourself. Then measure the second toys' scarf using cubes. Emphasise the importance of lining the first cube up right at the edge of the scarf.
● Write down the measurements of each scarf.
● Help the children to interpret the information gathered and then label the scarves correctly – longest and shortest.

Paired work

● Give each pair of children two toys. Ask them to measure the toys' scarves with cubes and then label them longest/shortest.
● Work alongside the children encouraging them to describe what they are doing. Encourage accurate work and offer support as required.

Plenary

● Pick one of the children to measure a scarf using a different non-standard unit such as paperclips. Ask the children to consider why it is so important to line the first paperclip at the edge of the scarf.
● Pick a child to measure a second scarf with paperclips. Select a child to label the scarves longest/shortest.

Potential difficulties	Further support
Children find it difficult to understand and use correct mathematical vocabulary.	Provide further opportunities for children to make direct comparison of lengths. For example, *Find 4 things longer than this pencil.*

Moving On
● Challenge the children to work out which of a set of four toys is wearing the longest scarf.
● Show children how to measure the scarves in centimetres with a ruler.

Who has the longest scarf?

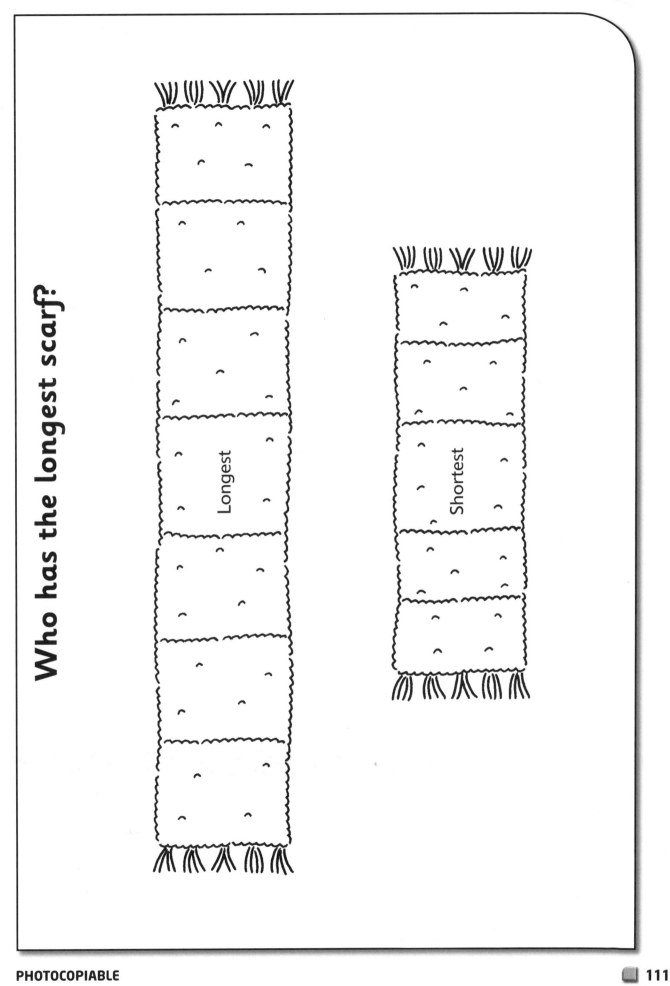

Longest

Shortest

Are we nearly there yet?

Learning objectives
(Y1) Read the time to the hour on analogue clocks.
(Y1) Solve simple problems set in 'real life' contexts.

Mental starter
See the starter 8 on page 12.

You will need
A copy of photocopiable page 113 per child; 12 clock faces set to o'clock times from 1 o'clock to 12 o'clock; 8 toys wearing stickers showing different o'clock times.

Whole class work
● Ask the children to help you arrange the clocks in order starting with 1 o'clock. Count along the line of clocks in 'hours' from 1 o'clock to 12 o'clock.
● Ask questions such as: *What time will it be an hour later than 12 o'clock?; It is 4 o'clock now, what time will it be in 3 hours?* Check the children's methods with them.

Group work
● Show the group two of the toys. Explain that the sticker on each toy shows what time they arrived at school. Say: *This teddy arrived at 3 o'clock and this teddy arrived at 12 o'clock, which teddy arrived at school first? How do you know?* Repeat for other pairs of toys.
● Now hold up two of the toys. Explain that they both travelled to school by train and you want to find out which of their journeys took the longest time.
● Say that the first toy left at 2 o'clock and arrived at school at 4 o'clock. Locate both of these times on the number line and demonstrate how to work out the length of the journey by counting up from the smaller to the larger number.
● Describe how the second toy left at 1 o'clock and arrived at 4 o'clock. Ask the children to count on to find out how long the journey took and explain how they did this. Together, work out which toy had the longest journey from the information gathered.

Independent work
● Give each child a copy of photocopiable page 113. Explain that you would like them to find out which person had the longest train journey. Encourage them to use the 12 displayed clocks to work out the duration of each journey
● Talk to children while they are engaged in the activity. Ask them to explain what they are doing and how this is going to help them solve the problem.

Plenary
● Set the class a time problem. Choose a child to explain what information they needed to use to work out the answer and to describe the method they used. Did anyone solve the problem in a different way?

Potential difficulties	Further support
Children are unable to read o'clock times.	See 'What's the Time Mr Wolf?' on page 118.
Children are unable to compare two times and say which is later or earlier.	Reinforce 'time' vocabulary in everyday contexts.

Moving On
● Make a time number line using digital clock faces or analogue clock faces set to half past the hour. Set simple problems for the group to solve.

Are we nearly there yet?

■ Who had the longest journey?

I left at 3 o'clock.
I arrived at 6 o'clock.

Joanne   Total journey time

☐ hours

I left at 9 o'clock.
I arrived at 11 o'clock.

Harry   Total journey time

☐ hours

I left at 5 o'clock.
I arrived at 10 o'clock.

Chloe   Total journey time

☐ hours

I left at 4 o'clock.
I arrived at 8 o'clock.

James   Total journey time

☐ hours

I left at 2 o'clock.
I arrived at 9 o'clock.

Holly   Total journey time

☐ hours

I left at 10 o'clock.
I arrived at 1 o'clock.

Tom   Total journey time

☐ hours

What's your favourite?

Learning objectives
(Y1) Solve a given problem by sorting, classifying and organising information in simple ways. Discuss and explain results.

Mental starter
See the starter 22 on page 17.

You will need
The question cards from photocopiable page 115 (1 set for group work and 1 set per 3 children); several small boxes; different coloured cubes (red, yellow, green, blue, pink, black).

Whole class work

● Explain that you are all going to find out which is the most popular colour in the class.
● Invite each child to put their favourite colour cube in a box. Ask the children to suggest how to arrange the cubes in order to make it easier to count and compare them.
● Show the children how to build cubes of the same colour into towers. Invite individuals to count how many children like each colour.
● Ask the children to say which colour is the most popular and how they know this.

Group work

Read the questions from the cards (cut out from photocopiable page 115). Ask the children to answer each question by interpreting the information represented by the towers of cubes (see whole class work, above). Provide support as necessary. Encourage the children to explain how they worked the answer out.
● Divide the group into threes. Give each group of children a box containing 20 coloured cubes and a photocopiable sheet. Explain that the cubes in the box represent the favourite colours of a different group of children. Ask the children to use the cubes to help them answer the questions on the sheet.
● Observe the children. Do they organise the cubes before trying to answer the questions? If not, intervene and tell them to organise the cubes into towers to make the information easier to interpret.

Plenary

Have a simple discussion to assess the group's understanding of how a simple problem can be solved by collecting, organising and interpreting information. Ask: *What did we want to find out? How did we collect the information? Could we have done it another way? Why did we organise the cubes into towers? How did we know which colour was the most/ least popular?*

Potential difficulties	Further support
Children cannot work out how many more children like one colour than another.	Make two towers the same height by breaking the 'extra' cubes off the taller one. Explain that these cubes represent 'how many more' children like one colour than the other.
Children do not understand that each cube represents the opinion of one child.	Make a 'human block graph' (see 'Party food', page 116).

Moving On
● Show children how to represent the data in the form of a pictogram or block graph.
● Ask the children to carry out a similar investigation independently, such as: *What is the most common eye colour in the class?*

Name _____

What's your favourite?

Which colour is the most popular?

How many children like red best?

How many children like green best?

Which colour is the least popular?

How many more children like blue than yellow?

How many more children like red than black?

How many children took part in the survey altogether?

How many more children like pink than black?

Party food

Learning objective
(Y1) Solve a given problem by sorting, classifying and organising information in simple ways. Discuss and explain the results.

Mental starter
See the starter 45 on page 25.

You will need
A copy of photocopiable page 117 for each child in the group; A4 labels - 'lemon', 'orange', 'strawberry' and 'lime'; a teddy; green, red, orange and yellow interlocking cubes.

Whole class work

● Tell the children that it is Teddy's birthday next week and that he is having a party to celebrate. He would like the children to help him decide what flavour jelly to serve at the party.
● Hold up each of the labels to show the class the choice of flavours. Ask the children to suggest how they could quickly collect the information needed. How could the information be recorded? (Hopefully the children will suggest putting their hands up to vote and recording the information in a table or as a tally.)
● Collect and record the information using one of the methods suggested by the class.
● Ask the class to look at the results and say which flavour jelly was the most popular.

Group work

● Explain to the less able group that you are going to help them to make a more visual representation of the preferred jelly flavours.
● Ask how many children picked lime jelly. Give the child who answers correctly some green cubes and tell them to make a tower to represent all the children who picked that flavour. Repeat this process for the other three flavours.
● Stand the towers side by side. Pose a variety of simple questions that require the children to interpret the information represented by the towers. For example: *How many children think that Teddy should serve strawberry jelly?; How many more children have picked orange jelly than lime jelly?*

Independent work

● Give each child in the less able group a copy of photocopiable page 117. Ask them to colour in the correct number of jellies in each column to create a simple pictogram.

Plenary

● Pick a child from the less able group to tell Teddy which jelly they think he should serve at his party.
● Ask specific children to explain to Teddy how the decision was reached. How did they collect the information? How was the information sorted and recorded?
● Ask one of children to talk about their pictogram. Can they explain what it shows?

Moving On
● Ask the children to carry out a similar investigation more independently, recording the information using their own preferred method. Set a question such as: *Which game should teddy play at his party?*

Potential difficulties	Further support
The class are unable to suggest a suitable method of collecting the information needed to solve the problem.	Demonstrate how to make a tally chart.
Children find it difficult to explain their methods and reasoning.	Use scaffold questioning: *What was the first thing we did? Why did we do that?*

Party food

🔳 Which jelly do you think Teddy should serve at his party?

| | lime | lemon | orange | strawberry |

What's the time Mr Wolf?

Learning objectives
(Y1) Understand and use the vocabulary related to time.
(Y1) Read the time to the hour on analogue clocks.

Mental starter
See the starter, 4 on page 11.

You will need
The clock cards from photocopiable page 119; large number cards 1-12; a skipping rope; an analogue clock; a simple wolf headband; a bag.

Whole class work

● Create a human clock. Arrange the number cards on the floor to represent a giant clock face. Select a child to stand in the middle, holding the skipping rope two thirds of the way along its length. Choose two children to hold the ends of the rope to create both the minute and the hour hand.

● Explain that whenever the minute hand is pointing to the number 12 the time is *o'clock* according to which hour the hour hand is pointing to. Move the hands to show 3 o'clock.

● Look at a real clock. Ask the children to comment on the movement of the hands' speed and direction.

● Explain that the minute hand moves more quickly than the hour hand. In the time it takes the minute hand to turn all the way round the clock and back to 12, the hour hand only moves on to the next number.

● On the class human clock, change the time to 4 o'clock. Ensure that the hour hand moves very slowly so that it reaches the 4 at exactly the same time as the minute hand reaches the 12.

● Repeat to make other o'clock times.

Group work

● Play 'What's the time Mr Wolf Bingo' with the less able learners. Ask one child to wear the headband and be the wolf (bingo caller). Give each child in the group a shuffled set of clock cards and instruct each child to deal four cards face up in front of them.

● Start a chorus of 'What's the time Mr Wolf?'. The wolf must take a clock card out of the bag and read the time. Anyone who has a matching clock in their set of clock cards should turn it face down.

● The winner is the first player to turn all their clocks over and shout *Dinner time!*

Plenary

● Hold up the analogue clock showing 4 o'clock. Ask the children to say what time the clock is showing. Discuss the difference between the minute and the hour hand.

● Repeat with other o'clock times.

Potential difficulties	Further support
Children confuse the minute and hour hands.	Label the 'hands' during the whole-class activity. Let children colour the minute and hour hands two different colours on their clock cards to help them to differentiate between them.

Moving On
● Set simple word problems such as: *I had my tea at 6 o'clock. I went to bed 1 hour later. What time did I go to bed?*
● Adapt the whole class work to teach children to read times to the half-hour.

What's the time Mr Wolf?

Where's the bear?

Learning objective
(Y1) Use everyday language to describe position.

Mental starter
See the starter 38 on page 23.

You will need
A set of positional vocabulary cards; photocopiable page 121; a large box and a large teddy; a small box and a small toy for every child in the class; paper and pencils.

Whole class work

● Ask the children to sit in a circle. Put the large box in the centre of the circle and a small box and small toy in front of each child.
● Put the large teddy under the box. Ask: *Where's the bear?* Encourage the children to tell you the position of the teddy using positional language. Once a child has answered correctly, reinforce the appropriate vocabulary by instructing all the children to place their own toy in the same position.
● Repeat this activity for each of the positions described on the cards on photocopiable page 121.
● Finally, hold up and read out each card in turn. Ask the children to race to be first to place their toy in the correct position each time.

Group work

● Work with a group of less able children. Shuffle the vocabulary cards and place them face down on the table. Instruct the children to put their toys in a position relative to their box. Turn over the top card and read it out. Anyone who has placed their bear in this position scores a point.
● Record the scores in the form of a tally. The winner is the player with the most points when you decide the game is over.
● Finally give each child a piece of paper. Ask them to draw a box and then draw a toy in a position relative to the box.
● Ask the children to share their finished pictures with the rest of the group, saying out loud the position they have drawn their toy in.

Plenary

● Pick a child from the less able group to take a vocabulary card and say out loud the position of the toy. The rest of the group should place their toy in that position.
● Watch for any children who are still struggling; you may need to revise the vocabulary cards with them again.

Potential difficulties	Further support
Children have difficulty remembering the meaning of new vocabulary.	Introduce the vocabulary cards over a series of lessons.
Children do not remember and use the appropriate vocabulary when describing position in different contexts.	Reinforce children's understanding of and ability to use positional vocabulary in everyday activities. For example, direct children to move to different positions in PE – *Stand behind the bench, Sit inside the hoop* and so on.

Moving On
● Introduce other positional vocabulary such as: *higher than, lower than, further away from, at the edge* and so on.
● Ask children to describe the position or simple journey of the teddy on a floor map.

Where's the bear?

under

behind

inside

on

next to

in front

LESSON 48

Musical shapes

Learning objective
(Y1) Use everyday language to describe features of familiar 3D and 2D shapes.

Mental starter
See the starter, 15 on page 14.

You will need
The 'Musical shape spinner' from photocopiable page 123; a feely bag containing a selection of 2D shapes with curved/straight sides; two sorting hoops labelled with the 'straight' and 'curved' vocabulary cards from photocopiable page 123; a CD or tape player and a lively piece of music.

Whole class work
● Ask the class to sit in a straight line. Draw and label a straight line on the board. Now ask them to sit in a line curved like a rainbow. Draw and label a curved line.
● Spin the 'musical shapes' spinner. Call out *Straight* or *Curved* according to what the spinner lands on. The children should trace an appropriate line in the air with their finger. Alternatively, allow the children to stand up and move around the room on a curved/straight pathway.
● Let all the children have a turn to spin the spinner and call out an instruction for the others to follow.

Group work
● Play 'Musical shapes' with the less able group. Organise the group so that they are sitting in a circle on the floor. Put the labelled sorting hoops in the centre of the circle.
● Ask the children to pass the feely bag of shapes around the circle while the music plays. When the music stops choose a child to spin the spinner and call out *Straight* or *Curved*. The child holding the feely bag must feel inside the bag for a corresponding shape and place it in the correct hoop.
● Continue until all of the objects from the bag have been classified

Paired work
● Divide the less able group into pairs. Ask them to walk around the classroom together looking for curved and straight lines in their surroundings.
● Talk to each pair about the examples of straight and curved lines they have identified.

Plenary
● Ask the group of less able learners to sit in a circle again.
● Place the 2D shapes in the centre of the circle. Describe one of the shapes and ask for a volunteer to point to a shape that matches the description. Tell the child who answers correctly to describe a shape to someone else until everyone has had a turn to guess and describe.

Potential difficulties	Further support
Children find it difficult to understand and use correct mathematical vocabulary.	Use and reinforce key vocabulary in other contexts. For example, *Which of these letters are made up from straight/curved lines (or both)?*
Children are unable to differentiate between straight and curved sides.	Make straight and curved lines in the sand or with finger paints. Play 'Follow-my-leader'. Move along straight and curved pathways.

Moving On
● Sort flat shapes in an overlapping Venn diagram according to whether they have straight, curved or both straight and curved sides.
● Show children how to count the number of sides a shape has.

Musical shapes

▪ Copy the spinner onto thin card. Cut out

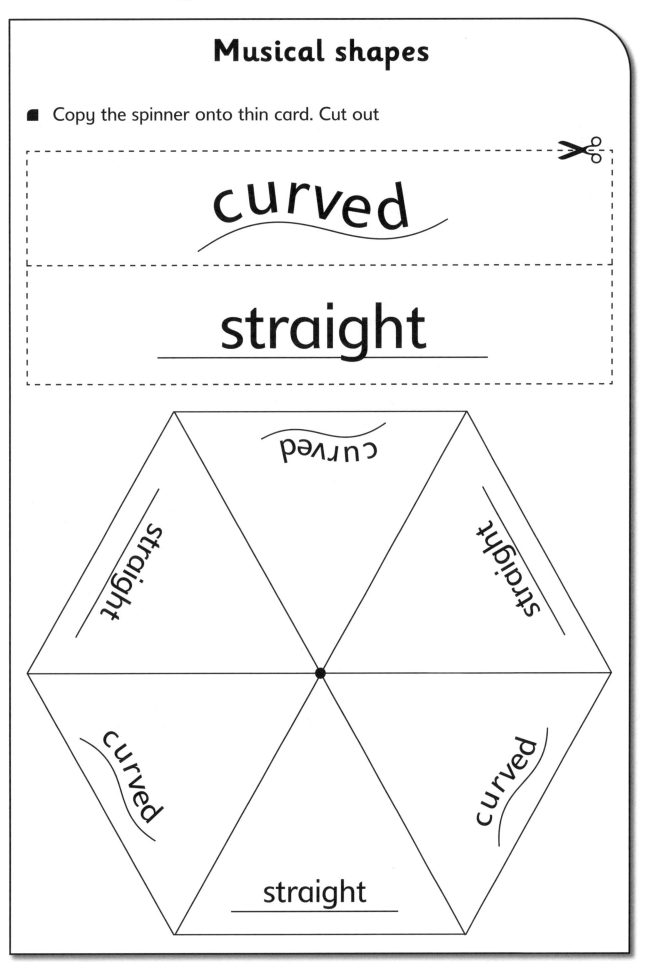

Counting corners

Learning objectives
(Y1) Use everyday language to describe features of familiar 3D and 2D shapes.
(Y2) Sort shapes and describe some of their features.

Mental starter
See the starter 9 on page 12.

You will need
Two sets of 'Counting corners' cards made from photocopiable page 125 copied onto card (highlight one corner of each shape with a highlighter pen); a ball of string; a hat; pin boards; elastic bands; Blu-Tack.

Whole class work

● Ask the class to sit in a circle. Explain that you are going to create different shapes using the string.
● Give one child the ball of string. Instruct them to hold the loose end tightly and then roll the ball to someone further around the circle. Direct the receiving child to keep hold of the unravelling string and roll the ball on again. Finally send the ball of string back to the first child.
● Discuss the shape which has been created. Ask: *What is it called? Does it have straight or curved sides? What is this part of the shape called?* (A corner)
● Give the hat to one of the 'corners' to wear. Count the corners again, starting from the hat. Describe how by marking the first corner this helped you to know when to stop counting.
● Make a variety of shapes in this way. Count the corners on each shape.

Group work

● Provide the children in the group with pin boards and ask them to make some shapes.
● Ask them to count the number of corners each shape has. Show them how to mark one of the corners with some Blu-Tack to help them remember which corner they started counting from.
● Split the children into smaller groups or pairs. Show them how to use the 'Counting corners' cards to play a pairing game.
● Players take it in turns to turn over two cards. If the shapes pictured have an equal number of corners they may keep them. The winner is the player who collects the most pairs. Encourage the children to count the corners accurately by starting from the highlighted corner.

Plenary

Enlarge a set of the cards and do not highlight the corners. Write the headings 'two corners' and so on, on the board. Work with the less able group to sort all the shapes under the appropriate headings.
● Assess how quickly the group can sort all the shapes, focus on children who may be struggling.

Potential difficulties	Further support
Children have difficulty understanding and using correct mathematical vocabulary.	Reinforce key vocabulary in other contexts. Ask children to run to each corner of the playground.
Children cannot identify the corners on a 2D shape, such as a square.	Sort a set of irregular shapes into those which have corners and those which have no corners.

Moving On
● Ask the children to draw shapes on dotty paper with a specified number of corners.

Counting corners

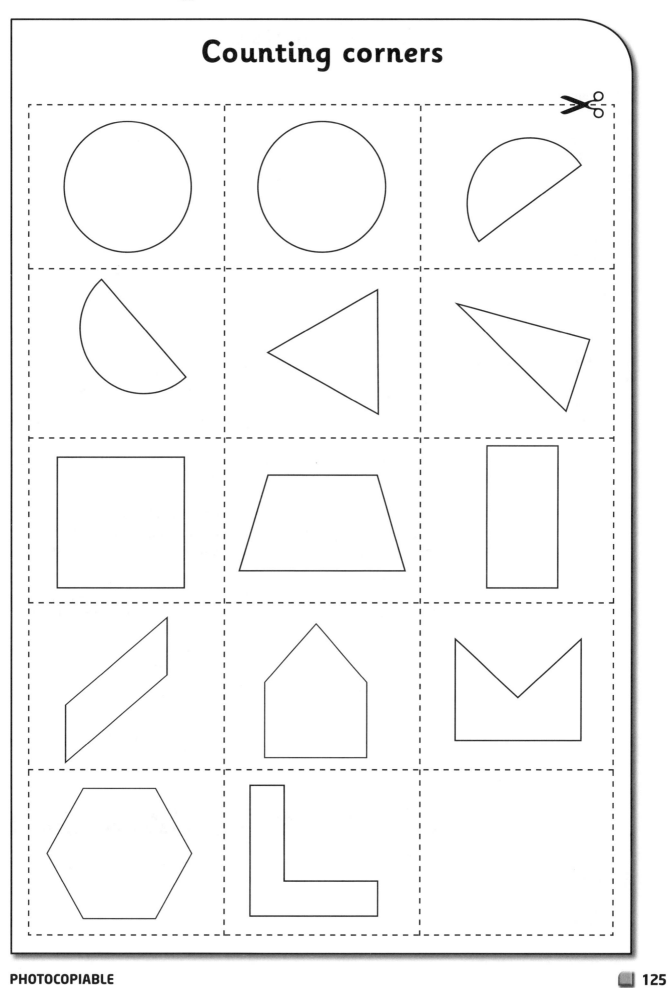

Cat and mouse

Learning objectives
(Y1) Use everyday language to describe position, direction and movement.
(Y1) Make whole turns and half turns.

Mental starter
See the starter 3 on page 10.

You will need
A copy of photocopiable page 127 per pair; 9 small mats; several dice labelled 1, 1, 1, 2, 2, 2; a clock; 1 (yellow) bean bag.

Whole class work

● Sing the 'Hokey Cokey' (traditional) together, doing the actions. Draw attention to the words, *turn around*. Repeat the action.
● Ask several children to describe the turn they made. Explain that when something turns all the way around once and ends up facing the same way it is called a whole turn.
● Provide a range of opportunities for children to practise making whole turns. For example, say: *On the count of 3 make a whole turn; Make the hands on this clock turn a whole turn.* And so on.
● Explain that when something turns around to face the opposite way it is called a half turn. Give the children opportunities to practise making half turns.

Group work

● Place the 9 mats in a line on the floor.
● Pick two children to be a cat and a mouse. Tell the cat to stand at one end of the track. Place a bean bag at the opposite end of the track to represent a piece of cheese. Direct the mouse to stand on the middle mat facing the cheese.
● The aim of the game is for the mouse to reach the cheese without being caught by the cat!
● Demonstrate how to determine the direction and distance the mouse may travel by rolling the dice, selecting a half/whole card from the pile (cards cut out from photocopiable page 127) and then instructing the mouse accordingly. For example, say: *Make a half turn and move forward 2 spaces.* The cat may either remain stationary, or one child could direct the cat with cards with the aim of catching the mouse!

Paired work

● Give each pair of children a game board and set of cards made from photocopiable page 127, and a dice. Tell them to decide who will be the mouse and who will be the cat.
● Play the game in the same way as the group activity. Each time the mouse lands on the cheese they win a point, but each time the cat catches the mouse that player wins a point The first player to get 6 points wins the game.

Plenary

● Assess whether the group have understood different positions, directions and movements by asking them to stand up and move according to verbal instructions.

Moving On
● Give more complex instructions such as *Make a whole turn clockwise.*
● Rotate different shapes and pictures through half a turn.

Potential difficulties	Further support
Children find it difficult to recognise/ make whole and half turns.	Provide other opportunities for children to make different turns themselves and to watch others making turns.

Cat and mouse

START

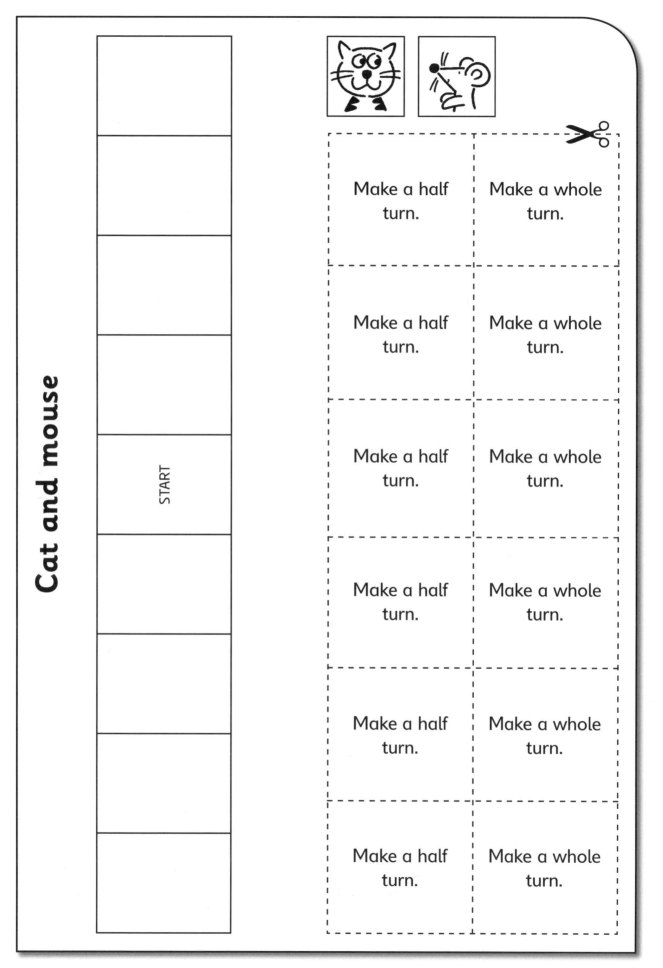

Make a half turn.	Make a whole turn.
Make a half turn.	Make a whole turn.
Make a half turn.	Make a whole turn.
Make a half turn.	Make a whole turn.
Make a half turn.	Make a whole turn.
Make a half turn.	Make a whole turn.

In this series:

ISBN 0-439-96519-5
ISBN 978-0439-96519-4

ISBN 0-439-965-209
ISBN 978-0439-96520-0

ISBN 0-439-96521-7
ISBN 978-0439-96521-7

Also available:

ISBN 0-439-97177-2
ISBN 978-0439-97177-5

ISBN 0-439-97178-0
ISBN 978-0439-97178-2

ISBN 0-439-97179-9
ISBN 978-0439-97179-9

To find out more, call: 0845 603 9091
or visit our website www.scholastic.co.uk